Praise for *Confronting Without Offending*

"I appreciate the reminder that it is possible to confront without offending. Deborah Pegues deals with this subject with an authority that is the result of extensive study and research. At the same time, the book is clear, easy to understand, and practical."

BISHOP CHARLES E. BLAKE,
Presiding Bishop of the International
Churches of God in Christ

"We will experience conflict in our lives, but few of us know what to do about it. Some of us try to control situations with angry outbursts, and some ignore festering problems in hopes they will go away. Deborah Pegues shows us how to manage conflict in a practical way without offending others. We all need this book!"

FLORENCE LITTAUER,
International speaker and
author of *PERSONALITY PLUS*

Confronting without Offending

Deborah Smith Pegues

HARVEST HOUSE PUBLISHERS

EUGENE, OREGON

CONFRONTING WITHOUT OFFENDING
Copyright © 2009 by Deborah Smith Pegues
Published by Harvest House Publishers
Eugene, Oregon 97402
www.harvesthousepublishers.com

Library of Congress Cataloging-in-Publication Data
Pegues, Deborah Smith, 1950-
Confronting without offending / Deborah Smith Pegues.
    p. cm.
Includes bibliographical references and index.
ISBN 978-0-7369-2149-7 (pbk.)
1. Conflict management—Religious aspects—Christianity. I. Title.
BV4597.53.C58P43 2009
248.4—dc22

                                                                    2008038742

Printed in the United States of America

09 10 11 12 13 14 15 16 17 / BP-SK / 10 9 8 7 6 5 4 3 2 1

This book is dedicated to the memory of Dr. H. Marvin Smith and his wife, Dr. Juanita Smith, former pastors of the West Adams Foursquare Church in Los Angeles, California.

As my spiritual mentors and cheerleaders, they were a model of generosity, faithfulness, forgiveness, and love. I am eternally grateful to God for allowing me the privilege of sitting under their ministry and witnessing real saints firsthand.

Acknowledgments

Thanks to all of my family and friends for their prayers, their conflict stories, and their suggestions that made the writing of this book possible. I am especially grateful to Harold and Ruth Kelley who encouraged me and shared their mountain retreat to create a perfect writing environment.

I also want to thank Pastor Edward Smith of the Zoe Christian Fellowship of Whittier, California, for his courage and commitment to teaching biblical principles of conflict management, and for using the earlier version of this book as a resource.

I am eternally grateful for my husband, Darnell Pegues, whose technical, emotional, and spiritual support were key to my completing this work.

Contents

Part 5:
Confrontation Guidelines for Selected Situations

Part I

Confrontation:
The Bridge to Harmony

The Goal
of Confrontation

I had it all planned. It wasn't a really big deal, but I knew that my husband, Darnell, would be pleasantly surprised when he saw how I had improved his workspace in our home office. He had talked about how inefficient it was for some time now.

Today wasn't the ideal time to break away from my writing schedule since my manuscript was due in a couple of days. But I had driven across town at the height of Los Angeles' rush hour to pick up a piece of custom glass that would complete the project. I had called his office and his cell phone several times to determine how much time I had to complete the surprise. He had not returned my calls. That was a little strange. He always calls back within minutes unless he's in a meeting.

I decided to call him on his cell phone when I knew for sure he would be en route home. Still no answer.

Now I was getting concerned. *Has there been an accident? Is he okay?* After what seemed an eternity, I heard him pull into the driveway. When I peeked out, I could see that he was talking on his cell phone. He proceeded to talk for another 45 minutes while remaining in the car.

Now I was getting angry! My imagination was running wild. *Why doesn't he come in and call the person on the house phone?* (After all, reception is very poor in our hilly area.) *Does he not want me to know who's on the call? Why hasn't he called me back in the last two hours?*

Well, he didn't have a clue that he was in such hot water. He finally came inside and explained that he had been talking to a close relative who was experiencing myriad distressing problems and that he had counseled and prayed with her. Yes, he had seen my calls pop up on his phone, but he couldn't find an opportune time to interrupt the conversation.

While I was familiar with and sympathetic to the situation, I was still upset. He had consciously put someone else's needs ahead of mine. That just doesn't happen in our household—almost 30 years of a good marriage attest (by the grace of God) to our having the right priorities toward each other. Teaching couples to put their spouses first—after God, of course—has been our soapbox.

"I'm supposed to be your top priority, and I could've been stranded somewhere," I said, trying to hide my anger and trying to employ the principles of conflict management I've taught over the past 30 years. Besides, I had planned the evening to allow only enough time to watch him be surprised with the office changes and to hear about his day and to tell him about mine—then back to writing. Now, I was more than an hour behind my schedule! He apologized profusely and was bewildered that I wasn't proud that he had invested so much time ministering to someone.

The next morning when we joined hands for our daily prayer of agreement, I prayed, "Lord, help me to release Darnell from this offense and to not allow a root of bitterness to form in me." When we finished praying, I said, "I was still smarting over that incident yesterday. I just wanted to pull the covers off Satan and expose his strategy to sow discord in our marriage."

After this confession, I felt our harmony was restored. Despite his hectic schedule that day, he called several times to show me that I was indeed his top priority. It became the joke of the day.

Every offense has the potential to cause a
permanent breach in a relationship.

But strife is no laughing matter. Perhaps you've fantasized about a relationship environment in your life where everyone flowed in total harmony—completely free of offenses and interpersonal conflict. Wake up! You're dreaming. It's time to deal with Reality 101. Problems and conflict are a fact of life.

God did not create us to be carbon copies of each other. Therefore, in any relationship—whether personal, business, social, or spiritual—thorny issues will arise. Jesus told His disciples, "It is impossible that no offenses should come" (Luke 17:1). If you allow yourself to get stuck in an offense, your relationship with the offender can never be the same. John Bevere, in his book *The Bait of Satan*, says, "No matter what the scenario is, we can divide all offended people into two major categories: 1) those who have been treated unjustly or 2) those who *believe* they have been treated unjustly."[1]

Every offense has the potential to cause a permanent breach in a relationship.

One of the meanings in the Greek for *offend* is "to entrap." An offense is Satan's trap to deprive you of meaningful and productive relationships. When offenses come, someone must take action to close the breach. I believe, according to the Scriptures, that this is done through *effective confrontation*. That's why I'm writing this book—to give guidance on how to confront effectively.

Most people are avoiders, unwilling to confront at all. Those who do confront most often do so ineffectively. Laree Kiely, professor of business communications at the University of Southern California Business School, said, "The problem is people have never really learned how to communicate with each other in straightforward ways without doing damage to their relationships, or negotiating their relationships so both have some room to change or some room to stay exactly the way they are."

In the following chapters I will show you how to use face-to-face confrontation to build a bridge between conflict and cooperation, between disharmony and harmony. Many shy away from it, but confrontation can be a powerful tool for personal growth and relationship enhancement when done the right way.

Volumes have been written about teamwork and cooperation; however, most of us do not really understand the power of unity from a spiritual perspective. The Scriptures declare that God literally *commands* a blessing at the place of unity:

> Behold, how good and how pleasant it is
> For brethren to dwell together in unity!...
> For there the LORD commanded the blessing—
> Life forevermore.
>
> (Psalm 133:1,3)

The attempt to build the Tower of Babel was a vivid demonstration of the power of unity. After the flood, God commanded the descendants of Noah to replenish the earth. Rather than disperse across the earth according to His mandate, they decided they would build a city and stay in one place. They also decided to build a skyscraper that would serve as a memorial to themselves. They were united in their objective, but God was obviously displeased with the project. Seeing the power and productivity of such a united effort, God knew that the sky was literally the limit for whatever they set their minds to do. He had to halt their progress.

> But the LORD came down to see the city and the tower that the men were building. The LORD said, "If as one people speaking the same language they have begun to do this, then nothing they plan to do will be impossible for them. Come, let us go down and confuse their language so they will not understand each other." So the LORD scattered them from there over all the earth, and they stopped building the city. That is why it was called Babel—because there the LORD confused the language of the whole world. From there the LORD scattered them over the face of the whole earth (Genesis 11:5-9 NIV).

Yes, God was impressed with their unity in building the tower—though its purpose was contrary to His will.

Once the builders were unable to communicate, they were unable to continue building. The lesson here is pretty obvious: If you cannot communicate, you cannot build—anything. You cannot build a marriage; you cannot build a church; you cannot build a business.

Effective communication is the foundation of all human endeavors. Therefore, you must be diligent to keep the door of communication open even in the face of conflict. The apostle Paul cautioned us to "make every effort to keep the unity of the Spirit through the bond of peace" (Ephesians 4:3 NIV). He also admonished, "If it is possible, as much as depends on you, live peaceably with all men" (Romans 12:18).

The challenge is clear. Each of us must make it our priority and personal responsibility to stay in harmony with our fellowman. Harmony is not just about creating a pleasant environment; it produces synergy. The best way to explain synergy is to say that a hand is much more effective than five fingers working independently. I tested this theory one day using dumbbells. I wanted to determine the maximum number of pounds each of my fingers could lift independently. Two pounds was the limit. I then tested my capability with my fingers working together. I rationalized that five fingers times two pounds each should yield a maximum of ten pounds. Not so. I lifted thirty-five pounds!

This is the kind of synergy referred to in Deuteronomy 32:30 when it speaks of one chasing a thousand and two putting ten thousand to flight. Logically, if one can impact a thousand, then two should be able to impact only two thousand. But such is the result of unity—we are ten times more effective when we join together. It's no wonder that Satan makes every attempt to keep us out of harmony. He knows that our unity will thwart his progress.

Confronting Versus Retaliating

The word *confrontation*, like the word *diet,* has gotten a bad rap.

Most of us associate diet with weight loss, hunger, and giving up our favorite foods. However, a diet is simply any plan of eating. Some diets are designed for weight gain, complexion clearing, and a host of other positive objectives. They are all diets. And so it is with confrontation. To begin to change your mind-set about confrontation and to embrace the concepts that you will encounter in subsequent chapters, you must abandon any negative, preconceived ideas about confrontation and focus on the true definition of the word. The prefix *con* means "together" or "with," and the root *fron* means "face; to stand or meet face-to-face." Confrontation is simply *the act of coming together face-to-face to resolve an issue.*

> Confrontation is godly and is mandated by the Lord; retaliation is ungodly and thus forbidden.

Many people want to know how my teaching on confrontation can be reconciled with Jesus' teaching on turning the other cheek. Jesus was admonishing His disciples to resist the urge to retaliate when He said, "To him who strikes you on the one cheek, offer the other also" (Luke 6:29). There is a vast difference between confrontation and retaliation. To *retaliate* is "to return the punishment." The Lord wants us to be so committed to not avenging a wrong that we would turn the other cheek.

Suppose you and another person you are in conflict with are sitting at a conference table and her foot keeps hitting your leg. She thinks she's resting her feet against the table base and has no idea that she's causing you discomfort and aggravation. To retaliate would be to kick her back; to confront would be to say, "You may not be aware of it, but you're kicking my leg."

Confrontation is godly and is mandated by the Lord; retaliation is ungodly and thus forbidden. Jesus admonished, "Take heed to yourselves. If your brother sins against you, rebuke him; and if he repents, forgive him" (Luke 17:3). In the context of this verse, to rebuke simply means to tell him to stop. Jesus pulled no punches here; His words are clear and unequivocal. He wants us to deal with relational problems through effective confrontation.

"Confronting Without Retaliating"
David Versus Saul

David had every reason to retaliate against King Saul. Ever since David had killed Goliath, the insecure king had pursued him as if he were a fugitive from justice. The problem was that the people had literally sung David's praises for defeating the giant, giving David credit for killing tens of thousands while ascribing only thousands to Saul. Saul reasoned that David's next ambition would surely be to take his throne—and that the only way to stop him was to kill him. David was forced to flee for his life.

Accompanied by a band of brave supporters, David hid in caves and other places of refuge. One night while in hot pursuit of David, Saul went into a cave to relieve himself. As fate would have it, David and his men were far back in the cave obscured from view. David crept up unnoticed and cut a piece off the king's robe. David's men urged him to kill his enemy, but David refused and would not allow the men to attack Saul. His conscience bothered him for even cutting the corner off the robe.

David passed up a prime opportunity to avenge himself against King Saul's relentless pursuit. Although he resisted the temptation to *retaliate,* he chose to *confront* him.

> Then David went out of the cave and called out to Saul, "My lord the king!" When Saul looked behind him, David bowed down and prostrated himself with his face to the ground. He said to Saul, "Why do you listen when men say, 'David is bent on harming you'? This day you have seen with your own eyes how the LORD delivered you into my hands in the cave. Some urged me to kill you, but I spared you; I said, 'I will not lift my hand against my master, because he is the

LORD's anointed.' See, my father, look at this piece of your robe in my hand! I cut off the corner of your robe but did not kill you. Now understand and recognize that I am not guilty of wrongdoing or rebellion. I have not wronged you, but you are hunting me down to take my life. May the LORD judge between you and me. And may the LORD avenge the wrongs you have done to me, but my hand will not touch you" (1 Samuel 24:8-12 NIV).

Giving him the benefit of the doubt, David sincerely desired to know why King Saul had chosen to listen to those who told him that he meant him harm. Frankly, it was not others who had inspired the king to his dire actions, but his own deep insecurity (1 Samuel 18:6-9). In the true fashion of a man after God's own heart, David never lost respect for the king's position of authority.

This is a good example to emulate if we ever have to confront someone in authority over us at church, at work, or at home. We must continue to respect and honor the person's position while seeking to gain an understanding and resolution of the problem—even when those around us are encouraging us to do otherwise. We are never to adopt a vengeful attitude or to take steps to retaliate against an offender in an interpersonal conflict. The apostle Paul reminds us, "Beloved, do not avenge yourselves, but rather give place to wrath; for it is written, 'Vengeance is mine, I will repay,' says the Lord" (Romans 12:19).

Your Challenge

If there is a conflict you need to confront, it's important that you have clarity on the purpose or desired outcome. Consider your true goal in confronting the problem. Do you wish someone to stop a negative behavior, start a positive behavior, or make other changes? Be clear on what you plan to request.

2

Commanded to Confront

Whenever you face an interpersonal conflict or a situation where someone's behavior is destructive to himself or others, you have to make three basic decisions:

- whether to confront
- when to confront
- how to confront (the words to use)

Perhaps you are asking, "Should I confront every offense?" Absolutely not! The Book of Proverbs counsels us:

> A man's wisdom gives him patience;
> it is to his glory to overlook an offense.
> (Proverbs 19:11 NIV)

I believe the operative word in this passage is *an*. In general, we would be wise to overlook the one-time insignificant slights, digs, and other annoyances that are a fact of everyday life. However, we cannot overlook a negative behavior *pattern*. Most people will choose to avoid a confrontation and in so doing, create even bigger relational and other problems.

As always, the answer to life's problems can be found in the Word of God. The Bible admonishes us to confront in three different situations:

- when we are offended
- when we are the offender
- when a brother or sister engages in sinful, self-destructive, or unwise behavior

In all three instances, we are commanded to take the initiative in dealing with the issue. Let's look at each one and see what the Scriptures say about them.

When We Are Offended

In Matthew 18:15, Jesus said, "Moreover if your brother sins against you, go and tell him his fault between you and him alone. If he hears you, you have gained your brother." This is a clear admonition to confront the offender. In the subsequent verses, Jesus gave further instructions for how to get others involved if the offending party does not listen to you. In this book, however, we will focus on dealing with only personal, individual confrontations.

Most Christians believe it is a sign of humility and godliness to suffer silently and to repress their anger when they are hurt or offended. Repressing your anger or frustration is unwise. Every repressed emotion gets expressed somewhere. Some people will eat too much; others may turn to alcohol or drugs; still others may shop or become workaholics in order to work through the frustration of not confronting.

The medical profession has many documented cases of illnesses rooted in resentment and unforgiveness. I sat with a woman at a Christian women's luncheon once who had suffered a stroke. When I asked her what led to her condition, she said she never spoke up when things bothered her. I have since interviewed a number of stroke victims, and their responses are almost identical—they consistently buried their anger and never spoke up when hurt or offended.

Paul admonishes us to be on guard against bitterness: "See to it that no one misses the grace of God and that no bitter root grows up to cause trouble and defile many" (Hebrews 12:15 NIV). Effective confrontation is by far one of the best safeguards against a root of bitterness. Bitterness is accumulated resentment; resentment is unresolved anger that has been "re-sent" or repressed rather than being put on the table and dealt with through effective confrontation. In order for anything to take root, it must be underneath the surface. We can prevent anger from getting a stronghold on us by not allowing it to go underground.

Some people have such low boiling points or so much repressed anger and frustration that they explode at the slightest provocation. I call this the "simmer and blow" syndrome. Obviously, this type of reaction does not fix the problem; it can only make it worse.

Christians who carry these emotions around become dysfunctional before they know it. Any dysfunctional behavior in a Christian is Satan's trap to keep him frustrated so that he will not fulfill his divine purpose.

> The person who is more spiritually mature is always the one who initiates the reconciliation.

When We Are the Offender

When we become aware that we have offended another, it is our responsibility to actively work toward reconciliation. Jesus said, "Therefore if you bring your gift to the altar, and there remember that your brother has something against you, leave your gift there before the altar, and go your way. First be reconciled to your brother, and then come and offer your gift" (Matthew 5:23-24).

When we sense that someone has started to avoid us or we feel a strain in our relationship, it's time to take action. My husband and I often challenge each other to model our conviction that the person who is more spiritually mature is always the one who initiates the reconciliation. Spiritually and emotionally immature people wait for others to build bridges to them.

When We Observe a Believer's Destructive Behavior

You may find yourself in a situation when you have to confront someone, not because his behavior is negatively affecting you but because it's having an undesirable effect on him or a group. The apostle Paul admonished the church at Galatia, "Dear brothers and sisters, if another Christian is overcome by some sin, you who are godly should gently and humbly help that person back onto the right path. And be careful not to fall into the same temptation yourself" (Galatians 6:1 NLT).

Most people gossip when they see a brother or sister overtaken in a fault or other ungodly behavior. Few confront. Now understand that Paul's admonition is directed to someone who has a relationship with the one who needs to be confronted. This passage is not a license for legalistic Christians to force their man-made rules onto naive new converts. I have seen babes in Christ become turned off toward the church because some unwise person confronted them about their outward appearance. Why not take the time to disciple such newcomers in the Word of God and to minister to their other needs first?

Earn the right to be heard. Once you establish yourself as a nonjudgmental and caring supporter, further admonition and correction of new converts may be unnecessary.

Regardless of a person's professed spiritual maturity, everyone is subject to falling into sin or unwise behavior. Therefore, when we see a brother or sister straying from the godly path, it is our Christian obligation to "restore such a one." No one has 20-20 vision when looking at himself; we all have blind spots. It often takes someone with objective, spiritual eyes to shine the light on our blindness.

When confronting someone about his destructive behavior, you can expect excuses and defensiveness. No one really relishes coming to grips with his faults, weaknesses, or shortcomings. It is a natural response to become defensive. Defensiveness helps us to protect ourselves against the pain of the truth. Expect it, and don't be turned off by it when you confront someone about his behavior.

Defensiveness helps us to protect ourselves
against the pain of the truth.

Job said, "How painful are honest words!" (Job 6:25 NIV). Many will either blame others for their actions or try to justify them. Biblical blamers include Eve ("the serpent made me do it" [Genesis 3:13]), Aaron ("you know how wicked these people are" [Exodus 32:22]), and countless others. Not everyone will respond as King David did when the prophet Nathan confronted him about sleeping with Bathsheba and then having her husband killed. He said, "I have sinned against the LORD" (2 Samuel 12:13 NIV).

Rejected Input

I have shipped many packages from our local post office, and a few of them have been returned, due primarily to insufficient postage, an improper address, or rejection by the addressee. Let's take a brief look at the application of each of these reasons as they relate to confrontation.

Insufficient postage is not paying or investing enough to send the package. When we give feedback on someone's behavior—especially in a nonwork environment—we need to earn the right to be heard. This means we have invested enough in the relationship for the person to know that we have a genuine concern for his well-being.

An *improper address* is not addressing the person in a positive manner. We use the wrong tone, show hostility, are judgmental, and any other approach that is a turn-off.

Rejection by addressee occurs when a person is not ready to receive our input due to psychological reasons or his unwillingness to face certain realities during this period of his life. When we get that "return to sender" notice, we need to understand that it is outside our realm

of influence. We've done our part. Now we need to pray for his recep-
tivity to the truth and for God to send across his path somebody he
will hear and heed.

"Stop Your Hypocrisy!"
Paul Versus Peter

Paul, a "Johnny-come-lately" apostle of our Lord, persecuted and
had many Christians killed before he submitted to God's call on his
life. Peter, on the other hand, had enjoyed a close relationship with
Jesus during His time on earth. Peter was a key figure in the early
church.

Paul observed that Peter was engaging in behavior that was destructive to the church, so he confronted him.

> But when Peter came to Antioch, I had to oppose him to his
> face, for what he did was very wrong. When he first arrived,
> he ate with the Gentile Christians, who were not circum-
> cised. But afterward, when some friends of James came, Peter
> wouldn't eat with the Gentiles anymore. He was afraid of
> criticism from these people who insisted on the necessity of
> circumcision. As a result, other Jewish Christians followed
> Peter's hypocrisy, and even Barnabas was led astray by their
> hypocrisy.
>
> When I saw that they were not following the truth of the gospel
> message, I said to Peter in front of all the others, "Since you,
> a Jew by birth, have discarded the Jewish laws and are living
> like a Gentile, why are you now trying to make these Gentiles
> follow the Jewish traditions?" (Galatians 2:11-14 NLT).

Paul knew that many followers emulate their leader. Therefore, a
leader walking in error must be confronted. Now some have said that
Paul was probably envious of Peter because of his status as an original
apostle, but this was not so. Paul simply wanted to see Peter and the
other leaders walk according to the truth of the gospel, which declared

that the Jewish laws were no longer in effect. There was now no difference between Jews and Gentiles. There was no need to prefer one group over the other.

Paul's opposing Peter "to his face" is a clear instance of a literal confrontation—that is, coming together face-to-face. Since Peter's offense was public, Paul publicly rebuked him. If public rebukes were practiced more today, perhaps we would have fewer instances of ungodly leadership.

Paul admonished us to confront any brother or sister overtaken in a fault. We are not to be intimidated by anyone's rank or background.

Your Challenge

As a reminder that you are to be the initiator of a godly confrontation whether you are the *offender* or the *offended*, write out Matthew 5:23-24 and 18:15 on an index card and commit the passages to memory.

"Therefore if you bring your gift to the altar, and there remember that your brother has something against you, leave your gift there before the altar, and go your way. First be reconciled to your brother, and then come and offer your gift" (Matthew 5:23-24).

"Moreover if your brother sins against you, go and tell him his fault between you and him alone. If he hears you, you have gained your brother" (Matthew 18:15).

Part 2

Biblical Confrontation and Conflict Management Styles

Everyone uses a certain style or a combination of styles in dealing with various issues that arise. These styles range from the dictatorial "do it my way" to the low self-esteem "have it your way." No particular style is exclusively good or bad. Circumstances will dictate which style is the best in a given situation.

In this section, we will look at the lessons we can learn from the various confrontation styles biblical characters resorted to in the face of conflicts or disagreements. In a later chapter, we will also look at how our personality temperament affects how we approach and respond to conflict.

3

The Dictator

"Do It My Way"

Some people handle conflict through charging, commanding, demanding, directing, imposing, mandating, ordering, proclaiming, ruling, calling the shots, and laying down the law. I call them Dictators. In this chapter, I will discuss what makes up and contributes to the Dictator style of handling conflict.

One of the signature songs of the legendary Frank Sinatra is the one in which he sings, "I did it my way." I don't know whether Mr. Sinatra was a Dictator, but this song almost perfectly represents the Dictator's mind-set. The "my way" style of managing conflict does not succumb to or show much regard for the opinions of others. A dissenting opinion is of no consequence to someone who resorts to this style, because maintaining a relationship with the offender is not his primary objective.

Even though a smart leader or supervisor desires to have things done his way, he understands that there is more than one way to accomplish the same goal. The ability to be flexible is a character trait that can reap big dividends.

The Dictator engages in win-lose confrontations. He uses his power or anger to win at the expense of the other person. In many circumstances, this style reflects emotional and professional immaturity.

> "A brother offended is harder to win than
> a strong city..." (Proverbs 18:19)

Some Dictators scream and yell and confront every perceived problem. They can be a real pain. You find yourself walking on eggshells around them for fear that you might offend them and set them off. I've seen managers in the workplace who resort to this type of behavior. They don't engender any loyalty from their subordinates and are often deeply resented. When we treat people with contempt and intimidation, we will not get the best from them. Know that

> A brother offended is harder to win than a strong city,
> And contentions are like the bars of a castle.
>   (Proverbs 18:19)

The Dictator style is no way to motivate employees. Threatening subordinates with the loss of their jobs or lack of promotions and raises will only cause them to become mediocre and do just enough to stay employed.

The Dictator Supervisor

When I held a high-visibility position at a Fortune 500 company, I was adamant about the quality of the correspondence that went out of my department. Although I had a superstar staff, I edited all staff memos in order to make them "better." One day, because time was of the essence, I quickly reviewed a memo in the presence of the writer and concluded that it conveyed the message and required no changes. I would have worded it a little differently, yet I simply stated that it was okay to send it. The woman who had written the memo was ecstatic. She said, "No changes? I can't believe it!" She was beaming. From that day forward, I made adjustments to staff memos only when it was absolutely necessary. The impact on morale was amazing. I learned something that I had not learned in business school: people need to feel that they exercise some control or authority in their environment. Does this mean that you become a compromising, anything-goes wimp? Heaven forbid! What it does mean is that you realize that by empowering those you have authority over, you build a loyal and winning team.

Nordstrom, the upscale department store, epitomizes the empowerment theory. The salesclerks have authority to exchange merchandise or to make refund decisions on the spot. They are rarely required to appeal to a higher level of management. All of the salesclerks are extremely personable and seem to love their jobs. It's a pleasure to shop there. On the other hand, I know of a young Dictator pastor who is too insecure to allow the leaders under him to make even minor decisions without first consulting him, and he's rarely available. He will never build strong leaders. He will constantly be surrounded by yes-men whom he has trained by his actions to show no initiative.

The Dictator Husband

The spiritually unwise husband who demands submission from his wife won't get it; he may get *obedience,* but not submission. Obedience is the performance of a request, but submission comes from the heart. If my husband were to insist that I iron his underwear, I may resent the request but faithfully do the ironing. I may then consciously or unconsciously manifest my resentment in other areas of the marriage, much to his bewilderment. He would wonder, *Why does she always have a headache when I want to be intimate?*

With submission, on the other hand, a wife demonstrates the right spirit and attitude as she obeys. I believe that a man *commands*, that is, *earns* submission by the way he treats his wife. No, I am not suggesting that wives exhibit a rebellious attitude when they do not wish to submit. I consider myself a submitted woman. My husband even brags that I am! However, every day I am perfecting the art of confronting problematic issues as they arise, rather than allowing the root of bitterness to spring up and defile me.

"When Dictating Is Best"
Jesus Cleanses the Temple

In spite of the problems with the Dictator style of managing conflict, it can sometimes be the wisest option. When the law is at stake, when you know for sure that you are right, when a decision must be made and you're the only one who can make it, or when tough love must be practiced for the good of all—then dictate! For example, if your drug-addicted child insists on bringing drugs into your home and creating a negative or threatening environment for others in the household, he must be clearly warned that his behavior will not be tolerated. We see Jesus resorting to this style when He cleansed the temple in Jerusalem:

> When they arrived back in Jerusalem, Jesus entered the Temple and began to drive out the people buying and selling animals for sacrifices. He knocked over the tables of the money changers and the chairs of those selling doves, and he stopped everyone from using the Temple as a marketplace. He said to them, "The Scriptures declare, 'My Temple will be called a house of prayer for all nations,' but you have turned it into a den of thieves" (Mark 11:15-17 NLT).

Jesus was on the warpath for the common good. He could not allow the merchants to desecrate the worship environment with their commercial activity. To have kept silent would have set a precedent that would ultimately have resulted in the deterioration of the temple. Compromise was out of the question.

My husband, Darnell, and I often host family and other gatherings in our home. As you would expect in any large family, not all of our family members or guests are Christians. Darnell is a very principled man and believes that as the head of our household, it is his responsibility to maintain the sanctity of our home. The general house rule of conduct is that no activity can be engaged in that would displease God, that is, no profanity, consumption of alcohol, and other worldly vices. Some guests have been turned off by his refusal to compromise.

I highly respect him for his stand. Unlike many Christians, he is not afraid to let his standards be known. He is not afraid that he might offend someone or do something that will make him unpopular.

Dictators Have Needs Too!

I'm from a large family. As the only female of us seven siblings, I usually get stuck arranging all gatherings and celebrations. Many years ago, my husband and I moved into a new house around the same time as my birthday. We were so exhausted from all the unpacking that we couldn't bring ourselves to plan a special celebration. On the Sunday afternoon of my birthday, a friend from my office and her husband dropped by to say hello. While they were there, one of my brothers also came by with his five-year-old daughter, Ashley, to wish me happy birthday. Of all my six brothers who live in the Los Angeles area, he was the only one who remembered my special day. We were all sitting on the patio, when I excused myself to go and make punch for everyone. Ashley followed me into the kitchen. She came over, leaned her head against me, and said, "Auntie Deborah, I feel so sorry for you that only five people came to your birthday party."

Now Ashley was used to big birthday parties. She could not relate to such a small gathering attempting to celebrate anything. I quickly corrected her, "Oh no, sweetheart, this isn't a party. These people just happened to stop by." She took a long look at me and said, "But you gotta feel bad 'cause there aren't enough people here to have any fun!"

Okay, so I felt bad that none of my other brothers acknowledged my birthday. Ashley was not going to let me play it off as something insignificant. Later, I told my family that I was disappointed that they had not remembered. They made up for it the next year with a nice showing at a restaurant.

It's pretty hard for Dictators to express their needs to others. They try to hide their vulnerabilities. Consequently, others often assume they need nothing and treat them accordingly. Yes, I'm often a Dictator, and you can see in this example the results of my not expressing my needs. Had I let my family members know how important it was to me, they probably would have been more conscientious about planning a celebration.

If you're a Dictator, spare yourself some pain, frustration, and resentment. Let others know that you too have needs.

Your Challenge

Are there any situations where you need to practice the Dictator style because moral values are at stake or the common good is being threatened?

Are there any situations where you need to stop practicing this style and start focusing on hearing and valuing the input of others?

Why not solicit a close, spiritual friend to monitor you in this area? Give him or her permission to offer you objective feedback on your behavior.

4

The Accommodator
"Have It Your Way"

In contrast to the Dictator personality, some people handle conflict by adapting, adjusting, conforming, indulging, obliging, pleasing, or accommodating the needs and wants of others. Accommodation is behavior that we learned in childhood. Little girls in particular are socialized at an early age to please others. One of my great pastimes is playing with children. Often, I've heard little girls at play threaten a noncomplying playmate with a warning such as, "I'm not going to be your friend." The alienated victim learns that not pleasing others affects the quality of her life—her playtime—and may have negative consequences. So she learns to comply with their wishes.

Burger King has a slogan we are all familiar with: "Have it your way." They will customize a burger to cater to our individual preferences. The obvious thinking is that if we please you, you'll prefer us; if we don't please you, you'll abandon us for the competition. Ironically, Burger King is not the winner in the fast-food franchise war—and you won't be a winner in the game of life if you are always seeking to please others. This is the lifestyle of the Accommodator.

The "have it your way" mind-set of the Accommodator is codependency at its worst. The fear of rejection, alienation, or abandonment is so great that confronting an interpersonal conflict is out of the question. The Accommodator wants to maintain the relationship at any cost, even at the cost of her own beliefs, values, peace of mind, personal time, or resources. She has low self-esteem and thus does not feel that she brings anything of real value to any relationship. Therefore, she goes to great lengths to be accepted by catering to the desires of others. The risk of confrontation is too great; acceptance is king.

> The Accommodator wants to maintain the relationship
> at any cost, even at the cost of her own beliefs,
> values, peace of mind, personal time, or resources.

Many Christians think that to suffer in silence is their laudable duty. After all, they rationalize, Jesus suffered on the cross and never said a mumbling word. They'd rather keep quiet for "peace sake," as they often say. They have defined peace as the absence of an argument. Unfortunately, when you fume, fret, or experience other forms of inner turmoil, you have not kept the peace. Yes, you have avoided an argument, but you have created an internal storm. Real peace must reside in you, and that starts with an effective confrontation of the issues.

The Accommodator Parent

I have observed many guilt-ridden single-parents who refuse to discipline a disobedient or wayward child for fear that he will shift his love and affection to the nonresident parent. The child, who is always seeking limits or boundaries for his behavior, never finds any from such a parent.

Such is the case with a woman I'll call Sally P. She is a single parent raising two spoiled teenage daughters. They show her little respect even though she sacrifices much for them. They spend the weekends with their father and view him as the good guy. Even though the father has pretty strong boundaries regarding their social and other activities, the girls respect him. Sally admits that she fears the loss of their affection. Even though she makes a feeble attempt to impose boundaries, she ultimately lets them have everything their way. Ironically, her self-sacrificing desire for love and acceptance never comes to fruition; instead, her efforts are met with disrespect. No one respects a wimp.

The Accommodator Supervisor

I have noticed in the workplace that a supervisor will often fail to confront an employee's negative behavior or poor performance to avoid the unpleasantness of a confrontation. This will demoralize the high performers and can cause the rest of the staff to become mediocre.

Accommodator supervisors often develop new rules and mandates that influence, inconvenience, or demoralize the entire staff, when they are actually targeted at one person the supervisor refuses to confront. I assure you that your staff will lose respect for you as a leader if you don't deal with problematic situations in a timely and mature manner.

As a supervisor or manager you are responsible for developing the skills and working relationships of your employees; avoiding a confrontation sets a bad example. Furthermore, unresolved problems distract you as well as your workers and hinder all from focusing on performance and meeting company objectives. Everybody loses. Once you establish a reputation for being able to confront and work through thorny issues, you'll gain the respect of your superiors, your peers, and your employees or staff.

I'm reminded of my three-year stint with a large aerospace company in southern California. When I took a high-profile management position, my subordinates had more experience than I and were all of a different ethnicity to boot. I decided that rather than being intimidated by these realities, I would conduct myself as the manager the company expected me to be.

I implemented the principles of effective confrontation from the very beginning. I admonished the staff to attempt to resolve their conflicts among themselves before presenting a problem to me. I also encouraged them to confront me without fear of repercussion. I applauded them when they did. I must confess that I never enjoyed being confronted, but I always experienced growth. Even after I left the company, several staff members came to my home and rehearsed confrontations they were planning to have with a manager or peer. It was a very rewarding experience.

"Have It Your Way"
Abram and Lot

The story of Abram and Lot sheds more light on the Accommodator style of resolving conflict. It is also an example of when accommodating is the wisest thing to do.

God had instructed Abram to leave his country and his family and go to an undesignated location. He promised to bless him and to make him a blessing to others. Abram was quick to obey. He packed up all his possessions and headed out with his wife, his nephew Lot, and his servants. They accumulated even more possessions en route to the Promised Land—so much, in fact, that there was not enough land to support them. Quarrels began to break out between Abram's herdsmen and the herdsmen of Lot.

> So Abram said to Lot, "Let's not have any quarreling between you and me, or between your herdsmen and mine, for we are brothers. Is not the whole land before you? Let's part company. If you go to the left, I'll go to the right; if you go to the right, I'll go to the left."
>
> Lot looked up and saw that the whole plain of the Jordan was well watered, like the garden of the LORD, like the land of Egypt, toward Zoar. (This was before the LORD destroyed Sodom and Gomorrah.) So Lot chose for himself the whole plain of the Jordan and set out toward the east. The two men parted company (Genesis 13:8-11 NIV).

How can one not love a guy like Abram? His generosity and his desire to avoid strife are endearing. He and his nephew had come through many toils and trials together since leaving their homeland, and the relationship remained intact. Oddly enough, Lot was not mentioned in God's great promise of abundance to the patriarch. God had blessed him simply because he was with Abram. Now the prosperity threatened to separate them.

Lot appeared to be a real taker. But Abram so valued their relationship that he gave him first choice to the most fertile land. You'd think that Lot would be so grateful to this loving senior citizen who had caused him to be blessed so abundantly that he would take the least desirable portion of the land. But no, he chose the well-watered plains of Jordan. Such a self-centered act would be enough to ruin most relationships. However, Abram's priority was not to accumulate material wealth but to fulfill the will of God.

Prosperity can separate the closest of kin. Just let Aunt Suzie or Uncle Joe pass away without a will and leave an extra dollar or two. Family members who have had a long history together will part company in the fight to get the largest share of the estate. Abram is a good example for us because he did not have a "scarcity mentality." The scarcity mentality says, "There is only enough for me. I will be disadvantaged if I share the blessing—or the glory, or the information, or the recipe, or whatever."

Stephen Covey, in his book *The Seven Habits of Highly Effective People,* explains that people with a scarcity mentality "see life as having only so much, as though there were only one pie out there. And if someone were to get a big piece of the pie, it would mean less for everybody else."[2] This mind-set is played out each day in businesses, in the church, and in families around the world.

But Abram had faith in God's promises. He knew he would get what was due him. Maintaining the relationship with Lot was more important than owning prime real estate. And through the surety of God's Word, we find that God reaffirmed His promises to Abram after Lot departed: "The LORD said to Abram after Lot had parted from him, 'Lift up your eyes from where you are and look north and south, east and west. All the land that you see I will give to you and your offspring forever'" (Genesis 13:14-15 NIV).

"The Eloquent Accommodator"
Aaron Versus the Multitude

The desire to please is not a modern-day phenomenon. When God charged Moses to lead the Israelites out of Egypt, Moses complained that he was inadequate for the job because he was not eloquent. "But Moses pleaded with the LORD, 'O Lord, I'm not very good with words. I never have been, and I'm not now, even though you have spoken to me. I get tongue-tied, and my words get tangled'" (Exodus 4:10 NLT). God assuaged Moses' fears by allowing Aaron, who was eloquent, to be his spokesperson.

In Exodus 32, the children of Israel had been delivered out of Egypt and were en route to the Promised Land. When God summoned Moses to Mount Sinai to give him the Law, Moses left Aaron in charge of the multitude. After Moses had been gone for forty days and nights, the Israelites became restless and impatient. And now we find this man-pleasing spirit dominating Aaron's leadership style and yielding dire results:

> When the people saw that Moses was so long in coming down from the mountain, they gathered around Aaron and said, "Come, make us gods who will go before us. As for this fellow Moses who brought us up out of Egypt, we don't know what has happened to him."

> Aaron answered them, "Take off the gold earrings that your wives, your sons and your daughters are wearing, and bring them to me." So all the people took off their earrings and brought them to Aaron. He took what they handed him and made it into an idol cast in the shape of a calf, fashioning it with a tool. Then they said, "These are your gods, O Israel, who brought you up out of Egypt."

> When Aaron saw this, he built an altar in front of the calf and announced, "Tomorrow there will be a festival to the LORD" (Exodus 32:1-5 NIV).

Notice that Aaron did not protest or offer any resistance to their sinful request. He did not wish to be unpopular.

Moses returned and confronted Aaron about what he had done: "What did these people do to you, that you led them into such great sin?" (Exodus 32:21 NIV).

Aaron, fearing Moses' anger and feeling caught between a rock and a hard place, responded, "Do not be angry, my lord...You know how prone these people are to evil" (v. 22 NIV). As a result of Aaron's allowing the Israelites to "have it their way," three thousand people died that day (vv. 27-28).

God is not shocked by our humanity; He
remembers that we are just dust.

The moral of this story is that by not standing firm and by not exercising tough love, we often cause the figurative "death" of others and sometimes ourselves, our goals, our destiny. You see, death is separation. The Accommodator often causes some to be separated from lessons of life they could have learned or may cause some to forfeit benefits they could have had, such as emotional and spiritual development, financial responsibility, personal independence, and eternal life, to name a few. One of the most tragic passages in the Bible is John 12:42-43 (NLT): "Many people did believe in him, however, including some of the Jewish leaders. But they wouldn't admit it for fear that the Pharisees would expel them from the synagogue. For they loved human praise more than the praise of God."

These leaders chose to reject Jesus rather than to risk alienation from the synagogue! The good news is that God does not hate nor refuse to use Accommodators. For even while Aaron was making the golden calf, God was making plans for him to become the high priest. In Exodus 28:2, God instructed Moses to "make holy garments for Aaron your brother, for glory and for beauty." A few chapters later, Aaron made the golden calf. God is not shocked by our humanity; He remembers that we are just dust. He knows that He has put in each of us the potential to be what He wants us to be. He focuses on what we will be—not what we are.

How to Stop Being an Accommodator

If being an Accommodator has affected the quality of your life or caused you to respond in ways that were not beneficial to another, consider the strategies below.

See Everyone on the Same Plane

Most people with low self-esteem view others in a hierarchy. All of the educated, beautiful, thin, wealthy, popular folks (or those in positions of authority) are at the top; the Accommodator sees himself on the bottom. He considers himself privileged to be in the company of such people. It is his honor to serve such worthy ones. He would never offend one of these people by saying no to any request, no matter how inconvenienced he may be in performing it.

God is not a respecter of people's social standing. He does not esteem one human being higher than another. He loves and views all men the same. In my attempt to become more like Him, I conscientiously refuse to exalt one person above another—and certainly not above myself. In my work as a CPA and financial consultant, I often interact with wealthy people, heads of well-known organizations, or other high-profile individuals. While I respect their positions, achievements, and contributions to society, I do not esteem them as more inherently valuable than any other persons I regularly interact with.

Once on a trip to Africa, I was greatly anticipating meeting a highly popular political figure. When I found out that the meeting was subject to terms that I found troublesome, I abandoned the idea without hesitation and immediately shifted my enthusiasm to an upcoming visit to the shantytowns where the disenfranchised Black majority resides. I know that such an attitude is a work of God's grace, and I am a grateful, delivered Accommodator.

Express Your Boundaries

Every piece of real estate has property lines that let us know the domain of the owner. Anyone who crosses the line without the owner's permission is a trespasser. Because an Accommodator often fails to express or make clear his "property lines" or boundaries, people constantly trespass on his rights.

When I first started teaching the concept of setting boundaries, I used to say that some people had no boundaries; however, as I interacted with more Accommodators, I came to realize that we all have limits beyond which we would prefer others not go. It's just that some people are afraid to express these boundaries for fear of rejection or alienation.

I know a tenderhearted Christian woman who is always ready to minister to any need presented to her. God has especially anointed her to pray for the sick and to encourage the distraught. The problem is that she does not express any of her boundaries. People call her all times of the night. They engage her in long conversations and counseling sessions. She complains to her family about these intrusions, but has never put a stop to them. Her daughter purchased an answering machine for her, but she rarely uses it. She'd rather continue to complain and allow her health to deteriorate from lack of rest than to risk possible alienation from those who take advantage of her.

I heard someone say that the first time someone uses you, shame on them. The second time, shame on you! I am a firm believer that you teach people how to treat you by what you tolerate. Yes, settle this thought in your spirit and repeat it often: *I teach people how to treat me by what I tolerate.*

For over a year I ran my accounting practice from my home. Because most of my clients knew I worked out of the house, many would call at irregular hours and on weekends. Finally, frustrated by their insensitivity to my personal life, I left a recorded message that said: "This phone is only answered Monday through Friday from 8:30 a.m. to 6:30 p.m." I realized that by answering the phone at odd hours, I had taught my clients that it was okay to call anytime. The moral of this story is: Do not create any monsters you don't plan to feed.

A new acquaintance called me very early in the mornings to encourage me to stay focused on writing this book. One day I said to her, "I really appreciate your calling to encourage me in writing the book.

I should tell you that I don't get up before 7:30 a.m. I do need the motivation, so please feel free to call me after that time." A boundary was set. She never called too early again.

How do you feel about people who violate one of your personal boundaries, such as showing up at your house without calling first? If it bothers you, you need to advise the offender the very first time it happens that you prefer advance notice: "Sally, it's so nice to see you. Please call before you come next time so that I can block out some quality time for our visit." A clear boundary is set.

The advice columnist "Dear Abby" once received a letter from "Had It in Arkansas," a woman who had a brother in prison who was calling her collect several times a week. He also would ask her to send money for personal items and to pay his court fines. In response, Abby told the woman to limit the collect calls to one a month and not to send her brother any money unless she could easily afford it.

I applaud Abby's response; it is similar to the one I would have given. This woman simply needed to set some boundaries. I would have tempered the response a little more with the following script for the confrontation with the brother: "Mark, I sympathize with your plight in being incarcerated. I'm sure this must be a trying experience. Because my family and I must live within a limited budget, I'm going to have to restrict our phone conversations to once each month. Let me know which day of the month you plan to call so that we can be sure to be home. I will attempt to write to you as often as I can. Also, as our budget allows, I will send you some money for stamps and so forth. We look forward to your release." Boundaries have been set!

"Boundaries with Consequences"
Jesus and the Rich Young Ruler

When a rich young ruler came to Jesus and asked him what the requirements were for inheriting eternal life, Jesus responded:

> "You know the commandments: 'Do not commit adultery,'
> 'Do not murder,' 'Do not steal,' 'Do not bear false witness,'
> 'Honor your father and your mother.'"

And he said, "All these things I have kept from my youth."

So when Jesus heard these things, He said to him, "You still lack one thing. Sell all that you have and distribute to the poor, and you will have treasure in heaven; and come, follow Me."

But when he heard this, he became very sorrowful, for he was very rich (Luke 18:20-23).

No doubt Jesus became very sorrowful also because He knew that the young man had made a bad decision. Unfortunately, Jesus could not compromise the requirements. Because riches had such a hold on this man, Jesus asked him to forsake all. This went beyond paying tithes, giving offerings, and helping others as the situation arose.

Before we criticize the ruler, let's take a moment to appreciate some aspects of his character. He was one in authority who had high moral values. Unlike a lot of today's leaders, he hadn't been associated with scandals and corruption. He believed he had kept all of the commandments from his youth. He cared about his spiritual life and his eternal destiny. He did not share the worldly concerns of the other rulers of that day who wouldn't confess the Lord for fear they should be put out of the synagogue (John 12:42). Following Jesus was not the popular thing to do, yet he was willing to suffer the alienation and the rejection of his peers. He simply had this one all-consuming attachment—his riches. And because Jesus wouldn't negotiate, he was going to have to forfeit eternal life!

Imagine the state of Christianity had Jesus been willing to compromise. We would all be trying to negotiate one little pet vice to hold on to. "Jesus, I'll do everything else You require, just let me keep my mistress, my gambling habit, my bitterness."

What about you? How firm are your boundaries? Do you often say yes when you really want to say no? Do others take liberties with your possessions? Please be warned that Accommodators are prone to developing a root of bitterness. They dislike themselves and experience low self-esteem for not being true to their own desires and wishes.

Consciously Value Your Intangible Assets

In accounting, there are two types of assets: tangible and intangible. The *tangible assets* have physical substance; that is, they can be seen and touched. Their values can be objectively determined by a qualified appraiser. Buildings, vehicles, furniture, equipment, and so forth fall into this category. The *intangible assets* present a more interesting valuation dilemma in that they have no physical substance; their value is derived from the rights or other future benefits they represent for the owner. The goodwill of a business is a typical example. Its worth cannot be seen with the physical eye, but the value exists nonetheless. Let me explain.

Many times when someone purchases an existing business, he will pay more for the business than the tangible assets are worth. Assume that Mr. X desires to purchase a local restaurant. The building and other equipment are appraised at $300,000; however, Mr. X is willing to pay $700,000 for the restaurant because it has been in business for over twenty years, owns unique recipes, and is a favorite gathering place throughout the region. He is willing to pay an extra $400,000 for this inherent *goodwill*. Mr. X has placed more value on the intangible than the tangible.

We are constantly bombarded with media messages that put the emphasis on the physical, and Christians have bought into the system. We put more value on physical beauty, possessions, and other temporal tangibles than such eternal intangibles as integrity, kindness, patience, impartiality, and faithfulness, to name a few. I challenge you to be a maverick and stop the madness!

Start right now. Make a list of your God-given intangibles. Meditate on each one and give it a high value. Here's a list of mine to get you started:

- In my social life, I don't discriminate between the haves and the have nots.
- I have a good understanding of the Bible.
- I love giving sacrificially and encourage others to do so.

- I have an optimistic attitude.
- I have a good sense of humor.
- I inspire and motivate anyone who wants to accomplish a goal.
- I am objective and unbiased; therefore, I am good at resolving conflict.
- I express my boundaries.

Stop now and make your own list:

My intangible assets:

_____

_____

_____

_____

_____

Now the world may not put as much stock in the above as you do, but remember—these assets are priceless intangibles. So the next time you're tempted to exalt someone else's tangibles, review your list and thank God for His wonderful gifts to you.

When Accommodating Is Best

Before we conclude that accommodating is always bad, let me remind you that it can sometimes be the wisest option. Such would be the case in the following instances:

- You have prayerfully concluded that you'd rather maintain the relationship "as is" than risk the possible consequences of a confrontation. This is how Abram dealt with Lot in the example given earlier in the chapter.

- You realize you are fighting a losing battle and probably will not prevail. This is especially true when the other person refuses to acknowledge an apparent blind spot.

- You have decided, as God did with the children of Israel, to allow the other person to experience the law of sowing and reaping so that he may learn a lesson: "So he gave them what they asked for, but sent a wasting disease upon them" (Psalms 106:15 NIV).

Boundaries are meant simply to help others
know how far they can go into our territory.

Your Challenge

Consider some areas in your current relationships where you're unconsciously or unintentionally teaching others that their negative or insensitive behavior toward you is acceptable. Ask God for a creative way to put an end to it, then set a deadline for doing so.

Also, as you begin to set boundaries, be careful not to go overboard and start to build walls. One of Satan's strategies is to have us go from one extreme to the other. Walls keep people out of our lives. This is not God's will. Boundaries are like fences with gates. We can allow entrance to others when we deem it wise and appropriate. Boundaries are meant simply to help others know how far they can go into our territory.

5

The Abdicator

"I'll Run Away"

Another way of handling conflict is embodied by the Abdicator. An Abdicator handles conflict through retreating, bowing out, quitting, stepping down, separating himself, dropping out, walking away, abandoning, resigning, surrendering, or yielding.

To abdicate is to relinquish power or responsibility. Renowned psychologist M. Scott Peck asserts in his book, *The Road Less Traveled*, that "the tendency to avoid problems...is the primary cause of all mental illness."[3]

If this is true, then the Abdicator is a prime candidate for a mental disorder.

The Abdicator avoids confrontation at any cost. He will withdraw from a situation rather than confront. He robs himself of the opportunity to experience the growth that results from working through issues.

> "The tendency to avoid problems...is the primary cause of all mental illness."—M. Scott Peck

When he is offended, the Abdicator leaves the church or the ministry where he volunteers—and doesn't tell anybody why. He makes no attempt to understand the motive or intentions of the one who offended him. He fails to realize that many times the person who offended him may be unaware that he did so and meant no ill will. If the Abdicator hadn't run away, he would have found out.

The Abdicator will often quit a job with little or no notice. A friend who had been working with a nonprofit organization told me she had become perturbed at how the director was running the program. One day she just quit, leaving her boss high and dry. The director was appalled at such short notice and begged her to tell her what prompted her to quit. She told me she never gave the woman an explanation. How unfortunate, irresponsible, and unprofessional. What was the worst that could have happened had she confronted the director early on? Perhaps, she would have been fired? I doubt it.

Pouting is another example of an Abdicator's behavior. The pouting wife retreats to silence rather than express her frustration in a spiritually mature way, leaving her husband to guess what is bothering her. Of course, men are guilty of this behavior also. You should never expect anyone to be a mind reader! Express what you need. Don't waste time being upset that he or she *should* know. Don't assume anything.

> Remember that you teach people how
> to treat you by what you tolerate.

When I speak to married couples, I admonish men and women alike to move from Shouldsville, the imaginary city where everything happens as it should. Ask for what you want. If his opening your car door is important to you—men, it's important to most women—then tell him that it would really make you happy if he did it. Don't resort to passive-aggressive silence as a means of striking back. Passive-aggressive behavior is against the will of God. Matthew 18:15 clearly admonishes us to "go and tell" the offender his fault.

A man who always succumbs to the silent treatment by begging his wife to tell him why she's pouting teaches her that this is an effective way to get his attention. Rather than ignoring her or catering to her, he could calmly ask, "What message are you trying to communicate to me by your silence? I really want to resolve and get beyond whatever the issue is." Remember that you teach people how to treat you by what you tolerate.

I've noticed when playing with small children that one of them, usually a girl, will often pout and withdraw from the rest if things aren't going her way. I have always admonished the other children to ignore the pouter. I can't afford to teach the pouter that her behavior will get results. Eventually, she comes out of it and joins us.

"An Abdicator's Resentment"
The Prodigal's Brother

Jesus told a parable of the prodigal son who squandered his inheritance on worldly living. After hitting rock bottom, he decided to repent and go home to his father where he could live well again. His father, delighted that his son had come to his senses, threw a party upon his arrival. The sensible, older son, who had never left his father and had served him well, was quite upset by the celebration.

> "But he was angry and would not go in. Therefore his father came out and pleaded with him. So he answered and said to his father, 'Lo, these many years I have been serving you; I never transgressed your commandment at any time; and yet you never gave me a young goat, that I might make merry with my friends. But as soon as this son of yours came, who has devoured your livelihood with harlots, you killed the fatted calf for him.' "And he said to him, 'Son, you are always with me, and all that I have is yours. It was right that we should make merry and be glad, for your brother was dead and is alive again, and was lost and is found'" (Luke 15:28-32).

The father was a wise man. Although the son said he felt unappreciated, the father didn't cater to his erroneous assessment by canceling the party. He simply explained to him that having the celebration was the right thing to do.

Many times you have to reach out to Abdicators—at least initially—to give them the opportunity to explain their pain or frustration. However, you should not cater to an Abdicator just to avoid the discomfort or unpleasantness of his pouting or silent treatment. Doing so creates an imbalance that will ultimately destroy the relationship anyway.

Further, you should not allow a person or group at odds with someone to dictate whether you should maintain a relationship with that person. When I was in college, my roommate, Belinda, and I pledged rival sororities. A few of my new sorority sisters were often perturbed that I continued my relationship with her and visited the "camp of the enemy." I choose to believe that my interests are broad enough to allow me to socialize with an alienated party and to engage that person in conversations that do not focus on the issues that divide him or her from my other friends. By continuing the relationship, I am in a better position to build a bridge of reconciliation when I have access to both sides.

You must be careful not to put pressure on anyone to choose sides just because you haven't been able or refuse to be reconciled to someone.

"The Accommodator, the Dictator, and the Abdicator"
Abram, Sarai, and Hagar

Sarai, Abram's wife, could no longer cope with her barrenness. It seemed as if God's promise to her that she would have a child was not going to come to pass. Perhaps she and Abram had misinterpreted God's words. Sarai had waited long enough. It was time to take matters into her own hands.[4] She told Abram to sleep with her maid, Hagar, and being the Accommodator that he was, he consented.

After becoming pregnant, Hagar developed a hostile attitude toward Sarai and began to despise her. Big mistake! One should be careful about offending a Dictator. In characteristic Dictator style, Sarai's response was swift and severe.

Then Sarai said to Abram, "This is all your fault! I put my servant into your arms, but now that she's pregnant she treats me with contempt. The LORD will show who's wrong—you or me!"

Abram replied, "Look, she is your servant, so deal with her as you see fit." Then Sarai treated Hagar so harshly that she finally ran away (Genesis 16:5-6 NLT).

Since Hagar had no financial means or emotional support from Abram, you would think that she would have humbled herself, repented of her insolent attitude, and begged Sarai's forgiveness. But no! Abdicators usually do not take responsibility for making a difference in their situations. She simply fled. In fact, *Hagar* means "flight." Thus, she was acting out her true nature. Of course, she probably felt that a discussion with Sarai would be futile. Most people fear a confrontation with a Dictator.

Surely Hagar, as the maid, had other responsibilities to the household. She did not stop to consider how abandoning such duties would affect anyone else. She just wanted to escape! The angel of the Lord found her on the roadside, near a spring in the desert, and instructed her to "return" and to "submit" to Sarai (Genesis 16:9). So she tucked her tail, swallowed her pride, and went back home.

The lessons we should learn from Hagar are threefold. First, we should learn to remain humble when God blesses us or raises us up to an advantageous position. Second, we need to put the blame on ourselves when we are cast out (as in fired, demoted, passed over for a promotion) because of our own actions. And third, we need to know that even when we mess up, God is still faithful to see us through the tough times and to bring us out victoriously.

When Abdicating Is Best

Abdicating or retreating is not always bad if it is temporary. Sometimes we need to pull back to allow ourselves to respond rationally and in accordance with the will of God. We often need to seek His guidance and to get in touch with our own emotions. Other times, we may realize that we do not have adequate information to have an effective confrontation. Now, some Christians will use such a retreat method as a cop-out and say, "I'm just praying about the situation." Months and even years later, they are still fuming and praying about it. Don't retreat longer than necessary.

Expressing Your Needs: The "I" Statement

The following exercise will help you to stop retreating when you should be expressing your needs. It will be helpful to anyone who has acted as an Abdicator—which is probably pretty much everyone, at some point—to see areas in his or her life where needs have not been addressed.

The "I" Statement

In developing our spiritual maturity, we must perfect the ability to express our needs, preferences, or desires to another in a nonaccusatory, nonblaming, and nonjudgmental manner. We do this through the use of an "I" statement, such as the following:

> I feel _____ (the
> emotion evoked by the offensive or hurtful behavior, for
> example, angry, annoyed, unappreciated, frustrated, disre-
> spected)
>
> when you _____.
> (specific, nonblaming, nonaccusatory, or nonjudgmental
> description of the behavior).
>
> I would prefer that you _____
> (exactly what you'd like to see happen).

Let's try a few situations to get into practice.

FRIEND TO FRIEND

The Mature Way: "I feel annoyed when you criticize the message on my answering machine. I would appreciate it if you would simply leave your message and refrain from judging the content or length of my recording."

The Wrong Way: "Why are you *always* so critical? Why can't you just leave a message on the answering machine like everyone else!"

WIFE TO HUSBAND

The Mature Way: "I really desire to feel pampered by you. When you ignore my dirty car, I don't feel so pampered. I would really appreciate it if you would take my car to the car wash sometimes."

The Wrong Way: "Do you ever think about anyone except yourself? Look at my car. It's filthy while your car sits there sparkling clean! What kind of a husband treats his wife like that?"

RELATIVE TO RELATIVE

The Mature Way: "I feel frustrated when you forget to tell me in advance about family events. Last-minute notices do not allow me the time to adjust my schedule. I would appreciate as much advance notice as possible so that I may plan to attend."

The Wrong Way: "Why do you people do everything at the last minute? Haven't you ever heard of the word P-L-A-N? I have a life. I can't just change my schedule at a moment's notice to attend these impromptu gatherings!"

SPOUSE TO SPOUSE

The Mature Way: "I felt really embarrassed when you corrected my grammar in front of those people tonight. Next time, I would appreciate it if you would correct me in private."

The Wrong Way: "Why are you so picky? You didn't have to try to make me look bad in front of those people. Their grammar isn't so perfect either. Besides, they understood what I was talking about, didn't they?"

The Mature Way: "I feel insignificant when I come home from work and you don't get up from the computer to greet me. I would be really pleased if you'd stop working long enough to interact with me for a few minutes."

The Wrong Way: "I guess that work is more important than I am. Why, you can't even break away from it long enough to say hello! I'm going to start acting the same way so that you can see how it feels to be ignored!"

Subordinate to Boss

The Mature Way: "I feel unappreciated when you individually praise or acknowledge everyone else's contribution to the project and say nothing about my efforts. Next time I'd like to know if my input is valued."

The Wrong Way: "I wish somebody would recognize my contribution to these projects. Why, everybody draws from my experience. And what do I get? Nothing!"

Summary

Notice that in each "Wrong Way" instance, the confronting party was either judging, blaming, or accusing the other of negative behavior, rather than calmly stating what behavior he or she would prefer. Such approaches are counterproductive when working at overcoming Abdicator attitudes.

We need to meditate upon and embrace Isaiah 50:4: "The Lord God has given me the tongue of the learned, that I should know how to speak a word in season to him who is weary." Let this Scripture be your filter for choosing your words in every confrontation. Yes, you can speak with "the tongue of the learned" and you will "speak a word in season"—the right words at the right time. You can stop abdicating your responsibility to express your needs.

Your Challenge

Using the model discussed in this chapter, write out an "I" statement for a situation you need to confront. If you cannot think of a personal issue, offer to help a friend or coworker develop such a statement for a conflict he needs to address.

6

The Collaborator
"Let's Find a Way"

Now we've come to my favorite conflict-management style—the Collaborator. Except for instances where wisdom necessitates that you dictate, accommodate, or abdicate, collaborating is the most effective way to resolve most conflicts. One who collaborates when dealing with conflicts does so by cooperating, joining forces, uniting, pulling together, participating, and colaboring.

Before we discuss the Collaborator, let's briefly discuss the person who confronts ineffectively, who attempts to focus on the problem through indirect means. His actions range from throwing hints, making subtle jokes or sarcastic remarks, or just talking to the air when the offender is within earshot. He hopes that the offender will get the message. But even if he gets the message, he won't appreciate the indirect approach.

Those who collaborate or work together toward a common purpose demonstrate spiritual and emotional maturity. Because the Collaborator cares about the relationship, the other person's well-being, or the organizational goals, he feels compelled to confront. He doesn't circle the airport on problematic issues; he lands the plane. He is emotionally balanced enough not to fear the reactions to or the consequences of a confrontation.

> People who confront directly know what they
> desire and are not afraid to pursue it.

People who confront directly know what they desire and are not afraid to pursue it. Collaborators are not intimidated by rank, education, possessions, or policies. They are emotionally secure. Christians should be the most secure and confident people in any situation, as the following two Scriptures remind us: "If God is for us, who can be against us?" (Romans 8:31), and "The LORD is my light and my salvation; whom shall I fear?" (Psalm 27:1).

"Asking for What You Want"
The Daughters of Zelophehad

The five daughters of Zelophehad provide a great model of how to conduct an effective confrontation. The Israelites were about to possess the Promised Land. The daughters of Zelophehad were well aware of the guidelines that had been established for allocating the land among the various tribes. However, they thought these laws, which allocated land only to men, were unfair since they denied them the ability to inherit their deceased father's property. They decided to confront Moses and the elders about the unfairness of the law.

> "Our father died in the wilderness; but he was not in the company of those who gathered together against the LORD, in company with Korah, but he died in his own sin; and he had no sons. Why should the name of our father be removed from among his family because he had no son? Give us a possession among our father's brothers" (Numbers 27:3-4).

Moses, not being a Dictator, brought their case before God. I love His response: "And the LORD spoke to Moses, saying: 'The daughters of Zelophehad speak what is right; you shall surely give them a possession of inheritance among their father's brothers, and cause the inheritance of their father to pass to them'" (Numbers 27:6-7).

These were some brave women who took matters into their own hands. They had no men in their lives to speak on their behalf—no father, no husbands, no brothers, and no sons. Yes, they had uncles, but it was unlikely that they would support the women in their request since they were asking for land that would, under the current plan, default to the uncles (v. 4).

We can learn several lessons from their actions.

LESSON ONE: They went directly to the people who could change the situation.

Already part of a multitude prone to grumbling, they could have easily gone throughout the camp mumbling and complaining about the inequities of their situation. (I've often wondered if they were the only ones in this predicament.) Their going before Moses and the entire congregation was tantamount to a congressional hearing, and not one they were summoned to, but one they called! It must have taken tremendous courage to be such trailblazers.

LESSON TWO: They were very clear about what they wanted.

Many times in a conflict, we don't articulate what we want to happen or to stop happening. Sometimes we don't quite know what we want and therefore confront prematurely. But this was not the case with the Zelophehad women. They wanted the same type of allocation their uncles had received.

Notice that there was no evidence of any hostility on their part; they simply asked for what they wanted. Confrontation does not have to be hostile!

LESSON THREE: They were not deterred by set policies or tradition.

Sure, God had given Moses the mandate to distribute the land only to those males who had been numbered (Numbers 26) and who would thus help conquer the Promised Land. The women weren't numbered. The daughters of Zelophehad were asking God to change the policy. Even God can be flexible when it comes to fulfilling His divine destiny.

How many times have you walked away disappointed upon hearing that something you've just requested is against company policy? Such a statement is always my cue to take my need to the next level of management. Don't be afraid to ask to be the exception to the policy. "You do not have because you do not ask" (James 4:2). I rarely take no for an answer. Perseverance is a good character trait worth developing. It also does wonders for your self-esteem and confidence. And besides, we will never receive some benefits or concessions unless we ask for them.

LESSON FOUR: They made their request at the appropriate time. We could minimize and even avoid potential conflicts if we would speak up while there's still time to take action.

> A prudent person foresees danger and takes precautions.
> The simpleton goes blindly on and suffers the consequences.
> (Proverbs 27:12 NLT)

The Zelophehad Five spoke up while they were still in the wilderness; the land had not even been conquered. There's nothing like prudent planning. We can't afford to sit around and assume that everyone is thinking about our welfare. After the raises are announced is not the time to petition your boss for your increase!

Our courage to confront can often improve the quality of life, not only for ourselves but for others as well. Not only were the daughters granted an inheritance in the Promised Land, but God also instructed Moses to change the rules for future generations.

> "And give the following instructions to the people of Israel:
> If a man dies and has no son, then give his inheritance to
> his daughters. And if he has no daughter either, transfer his
> inheritance to his brothers. If he has no brothers, give his
> inheritance to his father's brothers" (Numbers 27:8-10 NLT).

Aren't you glad that Moses was not a Dictator? He could have easily said, "Sorry, the policy is set. You women go back home and don't make any more trouble." Rather, he took the case to God, who made it clear He is for women's rights. It could have been many centuries before women could own land had it not been for these courageous daughters.

LESSON FIVE: The women maintained a win-win attitude. Just when they thought it safe to exhale after their major victory, they find that the conflict is not yet over. The uncles later sought to appeal the decision. The revised plan was not in their best interests. If the daughters of Zelophehad were to marry outside of the tribe, their land would increase the holdings of their husbands' tribes. Such dilution could not be allowed. Now it was back to the negotiating table, and God rendered another landmark decision:

> So Moses gave the Israelites this command from the LORD: "The claim of the men of the tribe of Joseph is legitimate. This is what the LORD commands concerning the daughters of Zelophehad: Let them marry anyone they like, as long as it is within their own ancestral tribe. None of the territorial land may pass from tribe to tribe, for all the land given to each tribe must remain within the tribe to which it was first allotted. The daughters throughout the tribes of Israel who are in line to inherit property must marry within their tribe, so that all the Israelites will keep their ancestral property. No grant of land may pass from one tribe to another; each tribe of Israel must keep its allotted portion of land."
>
> The daughters of Zelophehad did as the LORD commanded Moses. Mahlah, Tirzah, Hoglah, Milcah, and Noah all married cousins on their father's side (Numbers 36:5-11 NLT).

Had this situation occurred in today's litigious society, these women might have said, "Wait, a deal is a deal. This looks like a breach of contract. Call the attorneys!" But no, they demonstrated flexibility and a mutually satisfying agreement was reached.

In order to successfully resolve conflict where both sides have legitimate arguments, it is critical that all parties maintain win-win attitudes. Such was the case here. The daughters would still get their inheritance, and the uncles would not have to worry about dilution of the tribal inheritance.

"To Eat or Not to Eat Kosher"
Daniel Versus the King

When King Nebuchadnezzar of Babylonia (modern Iraq) besieged Jerusalem, he took many of the Jews captive. Among them were several handsome and intelligent young men of royal descent. They were immediately enrolled in a three-year training program that would equip them to serve the king. Their nutritional regimen included food and wine from the king's table.

Daniel, one of the captives, knew that a confrontation was inevitable because he had already purposed in his heart that he was not going to partake of any food or drink that was disallowed or improperly prepared according to God's law to the Israelites (Leviticus 11). Yes, the king had changed their names, but Daniel was not about to allow him to change his character nor his commitment to keeping God's commands.

So he looked for an alternate plan. He asked the supervisor if he and his three friends could follow a vegetarian diet instead of the royal menu. Of course this request put the supervisor in a precarious position, for his life would be at stake if any of the young men appeared malnourished. He disapproved of the idea at first, but finally agreed when Daniel asked him to give it a try for just ten days and to compare their physical appearance to the young men who ate the king's fare. "And at the end of ten days their features appeared better and fatter in flesh than all the young men who ate the portion of the king's delicacies. Thus the steward took away their portion of delicacies and the wine that they were to drink, and gave them vegetables" (Daniel 1:15-16).

Daniel's political savvy and spiritual maturity served him well in the land of his captivity. The wisdom and the respect with which he approached the supervisor with his request warrants closer examination. Though he had decided that he was not going to partake of the king's fare, he *requested* (v. 8) permission to follow the vegetarian diet instead. His humble approach assured the supervisor that Daniel respected his authority and was far from being rebellious.

Many Christians have been disdained and even disadvantaged in the workplace, not for their holy stand, but for *how* they communicated it to those in charge: "I don't attend parties where heathens are drinking!" Where is the wisdom in this?

Daniel demonstrated additional wisdom in offering a win-win *alternative* to the king's diet. Yet it's important to remember that it wasn't Daniel's astuteness that caused the supervisor to give his proposal a chance; it was God's *favor* (v. 9). While we may seek the highest level of competence and hone our communication and other skills to do a job well, in the final analysis it is God who gives us favor with man. We must never lose sight of this reality.

We must remember to ask God for such favor. He has often given me favor with people with whom I least expected it and with whom I even had an adversarial relationship. When I was promoted to a vice presidential post at a major entertainment conglomerate, my boss, who made the recommendation to the board of directors, had caused me much grief in the past. Yet God gave me favor with him at the right time to achieve His purpose. Who can figure God out?

> The king's heart is in the hand of the LORD,
> Like the rivers of water; He turns it wherever He wishes.
> (Proverbs 21:1)

Your Challenge

Consider what changes in your behavior would make you a better team player in your personal or professional circle of interaction. For example, do you need to be more respectful of authority, value the input of others, or communicate more clearly?

Part 3

Strategies for an
Effective Confrontation

7

Preparing for the Encounter

No one was born with an innate ability to confront interpersonal conflicts effectively. It's a skill that's learned and perfected through practice and patience. Just as a bodybuilder develops a great physique by using correct weight-lifting techniques, a great communicator must apply the right techniques to achieve the desired results in resolving conflicts. Of course, no athlete attempts to lift heavy weights or to engage in intense exercise without first warming up his muscles. The warm-up is critical to the workout as it minimizes the risk of injury and increases overall muscle performance.

> No one was born with an innate ability to confront interpersonal conflicts effectively.

And so it is with a confrontation. It is much like weight lifting in that it can be painful but beneficial when done correctly. It too needs a warm-up phase in order to minimize the risk of injury to emotions and relationships. This chapter is about the warm-up steps you must take to ensure that you achieve the purpose for the confrontation.

Establish the Right Purpose

The first step in preparing for a confrontation is to establish the right purpose for putting the issue on the table. The focus should be on achieving a better relationship or getting someone to stop doing something that is negatively affecting you, others, or himself. The goal should not be to tell someone off, to get something off your chest, or to run a guilt trip on the offender.

It is important to confront yourself first. Be honest about why you've decided to confront the issue. Do you have an ulterior motive or do you want to see a genuine change in behavior? Are you carrying another person's offense?

Ask yourself, "When this confrontation is over, what behavior do I want to see the offender change?" Remember that in an effective confrontation, you are looking for a desired outcome. Confronting and resolving an issue to God's glory must be the ultimate goal.

Select the Right Time and Place

There is a time for everything. There is a time to confront and a time not to confront. It takes wisdom and patience to wait for the appropriate time. You'll not want to confront right before lunch or at closing time or whenever the person is preoccupied with another matter. Confronting when the person is most receptive to a serious discussion takes some forethought and planning.

Wife, when your husband first comes home from work, give him space to settle in before you bombard him with the problems of the day. Husband, don't wait until you arrive at the event to tell your wife you don't like the outfit she's wearing. Tell her when she can do something about it!

Make every effort to confront a person when he is alone, just as Jesus commanded: "If your brother sins, go and show him his fault in private" (Matthew 18:15 NASB). Confronting someone in the presence of another can cause him to become defensive to save face.

Since the essence of confrontation is coming together face-to-face, telephone confrontations are not the most desirable. With call waiting features, incoming calls can interrupt the flow of conversation.

Direct personal contact allows you to observe the other person's facial expressions and to engage in more effective listening.

If you have something really heavy to tell someone, it's not a good idea to have the confrontation at his house or yours. You'll want to select a neutral location conducive to good conversation. It will be easier for the confronted to leave the scene if he becomes belligerent. There is always the possibility this could happen. Sometimes you have to temporarily lose people to win them later.

> He who rebukes a man will find more favor afterward
> Than he who flatters with the tongue.
>   (Proverbs 28:23)

We must be willing to take the risk.

Writing a letter may be better than a face-to-face confrontation if the person to be confronted has a strong personality and you feel certain that you won't be able to get a word in edgewise. I encourage letter writing only as the last resort.

Preparing for confrontation is almost as important as the confrontation itself. Confronting someone spontaneously or without any preparation might have disastrous results. Preparation allows you to look at the situation more clearly and not in the midst of an emotional moment, and this will most likely lead to a more effective encounter. Just remember that prayer is always the best preparation.

Your Challenge

As you prepare to confront an interpersonal conflict, it's important that you first deal with your negative emotions, such as anger or resentment. While you may deem them justifiable, if you do not release them by the power of the Holy Spirit, they will become a roadblock to achieving harmony. You must also refuse to succumb to the fear of addressing the issue lest you abandon the entire notion of initiating a confrontation.

Owning the Problem

Owning the problem is a key aspect of a confrontation. You must speak on your own behalf. You must explain how a person's behavior has affected *you* or how *you* perceive the issue. This is a straightforward approach that shows your strength. In the work environment, it is especially critical to describe the impact the problem is having on you as well as others.

> Not owning the problem when you have a problem
> with another person's behavior is a cowardly act.

I have seen people attempt to confront by saying, "Some people think you…" rather than "I've noticed that you…." Not owning the problem when you have a problem with another person's behavior is a cowardly act.

I once had to confront a young executive about his poor grammar. Senior management in the company had made comments about it, and it was hindering his career. Before I approached him, I purchased a grammar book. When I met with him, he immediately became defensive and asserted that management was unfair and that his grammar was fine. Because I had a genuine interest in his success, I told him that I agreed that his grammar needed improvement. I owned the problem. I gave him the book and encouraged him to use it. He later thanked me for how I had handled the matter.

Confrontations are never easy but can yield life-changing results.

"You're Hurting the Organization"
King Achish Versus David

After David killed Goliath, the people of Israel greatly esteemed him and showered him with accolades (1 Samuel 17–18). This angered Israel's king, Saul. He saw David as a threat to his throne and sought to kill him. Tired of hiding in caves and fleeing the wrath of the insecure king, David sought political asylum in the land of the Philistines. Even though he had killed their champion, David obtained the favor of Achish, the Philistine king, who allowed him and his band of 600 men to relocate their families to one of his cities (1 Samuel 27).

To convince the king of their loyalty to him, they pretended to conduct frequent raids on various Israelite cities. The truth was that they raided non-Israelite cities and never left anyone alive to contradict their claim that all the spoils they took were from the Israelites.

After they had been with Achish for quite some time, the Philistine army mobilized to wage war against Israel. When David and his men showed up for battle, the Philistine commanders immediately suspected their motives. They were appalled that King Achish could be so gullible. Didn't he realize that David could use this as an opportunity to get back into King Saul's good grace by turning on the Philistines in the battle? They were livid with the king.

> But the Philistine commanders demanded, "What are these Hebrews doing here?"
>
> And Achish told them, "This is David, the servant of King Saul of Israel. He's been with me for years, and I've never found a single fault in him from the day he arrived until today."
>
> But the Philistine commanders were angry. "Send him back

to the town you've given him!" they demanded. "He can't go
into the battle with us. What if he turns against us in battle
and becomes our adversary? Is there any better way for him
to reconcile himself with his master than by handing our
heads over to him?" (1 Samuel 29:3-4 NLT).

King Achish was in a predicament. He had to confront David, whom
he trusted, on behalf of his commanders, who wanted him dismissed.
He couldn't speak on his own behalf, for he didn't share their mistrust.
However, the cohesiveness of the entire army hung in the balance. The
king knew he had to do what was best for the organization.

So Achish finally summoned David and said to him, "I swear
by the LORD that you have been a trustworthy ally. I think
you should go with me into battle, for I've never found a
single flaw in you from the day you arrived until today. But
the other Philistine rulers won't hear of it. Please don't upset
them, but go back quietly" (1 Samuel 29:6-7 NLT).

Can't you see the hand of God rescuing David from his precarious
position? Imagine the future king of Israel with the blood of his own
people on his hands!

As a former corporate executive, I've found myself in a similar
plight on a few occasions. I've had subordinates who interacted with
me quite favorably, but they wreaked havoc on the department by
being in constant conflict with the rest of the staff. Eventually, I was
compelled to act in the best interests of the organization. When the
buck stops with us, we must always do what is best for the whole. One
bad apple really can spoil the whole bunch.

I can identify with the king's anguish as he tried to let David down
easy. "I've never found a single flaw in you from the day you arrived
until today. But the other Philistine rulers won't hear of it" (v. 6). David
then attempted to convince the king to let him stay—all to no avail:

"What have I done to deserve this treatment?" David
demanded. "What have you ever found in your servant, that
I can't go and fight the enemies of my lord the king?"

But Achish insisted, "As far as I'm concerned, you're as perfect as an angel of God. But the Philistine commanders are afraid to have you with them in the battle. Now get up early in the morning, and leave with your men as soon as it gets light."

So David and his men headed back into the land of the Philistines, while the Philistine army went on to Jezreel (1 Samuel 29:8-11 NLT).

This story provides two key conflict-management lessons.

LESSON ONE: Once we know we have made the right decision, we must not allow ourselves to be persuaded otherwise, not by emotions, not by personalities, and not by our personal desires. King Achish answered each of David's rebuttals in the same manner. He simply stated that David's presence would have a detrimental effect on the rest of the army. Therefore, he had to leave the battlefield. The king used the broken-record approach. This can be very effective when we must stand our ground.

LESSON TWO: Confrontation must be timely to minimize further negative impact. Although King Achish loved David, he addressed the problem of his presence before any real damage could be done.

Many times we tolerate a situation too long before we address it. Often, irreparable damage is done. I know of a church where the pastor allowed one strong-willed member to alienate every other key worker until almost all programs of the church ceased. The last I heard about this pastor, he was trying desperately to recruit the former members. They had all gone to greener, more worker-friendly pastures.

Your Challenge

Recall a time that you had difficulty owning a problem that caused a conflict. Why were you reluctant to do so? What consequences did you fear and why? What could have been the worst-case outcome?

9

Speaking the Right Words

Words are our tools of communication. They never die. They live on and on in the heart and mind of the hearer. To maintain harmonious relationships in every facet of our lives, we must learn to use words effectively. The Servant of the Lord, the Messiah, was especially equipped by God in this way, and I believe God also equips us to speak words that get the desired results:

> "The Lord GOD has given Me
> The tongue of the learned,
> That I should know how to speak
> A word in season to him who is weary.
> He awakens Me morning by morning,
> He awakens My ear
> To hear as the learned."
>
> (Isaiah 50:4)

Prayer is essential at this point. You must get God's mind and insight on the matter and seek Him for the exact words to use.

> So is my word that goes out from my mouth:
> It will not return to me empty,
> but will accomplish what I desire
> and achieve the purpose for which I sent it.
>
> (Isaiah 55:11 NIV)

Whatever words you decide to use, know that the tone of your delivery will determine how your words are received. Tone is the external manifestation of your current state of mind. If you are scowling on the inside, the scowl will attach to your words. If you are optimistic, your words will convey hope. It's that simple. That's why you must pray and ask God to purify your thoughts and cleanse you of all bitterness and misunderstanding. Only after God has purified your thoughts and helped you to put away your wrath are you ready to address the problematic behavior.

> Tone is the external manifestation
> of your current state of mind.

Be Specific

When confronting others, it's important to describe specifically what you have observed or experienced. Beating around the bush or circling the airport will sabotage the outcome. Such evasiveness may cause the point to be missed or may lead to a misunderstanding of what you are trying to say. If you are confronting Sally about her flirtatious behavior, it's not sufficient to tell her to use more wisdom around another woman's husband. You need to say, "Sally, I'm sure you meant no harm, but it was inappropriate for you to straighten Jim's tie as you did on Sunday." Sally deserves to know the specific charges being brought against her.

If your boss failed to inform you about a meeting that involved your department, you could say, "Mary, my being excluded from that meeting on Wednesday has caused some real problems. I'd like to discuss them with you." Then, go on to list specific consequences, such as inability to meet a deadline because of inadequate information. Talking in general terms is simply not effective. It also makes it easy for someone to deny any wrongdoing or to misinterpret the message.

Jenny's Story

Jenny, a pastor's wife, found herself in a dilemma. Susan, an attractive female parishioner, had developed a burden for the first family—more specifically, for Bob the pastor. She would bring him special gifts that often could not be shared by the family. She would call him at home occasionally for casual encouragement chats. Jenny grew increasingly uncomfortable with Susan's familiarity with her husband, but held her peace. She feared that Bob would get upset and accuse her of being insecure and neurotic. "Perhaps," Jenny mused, "my insecurity is working overtime since I've gained this extra weight." She prayed with her prayer partner who urged her to discuss the problem with Bob. Of course, Bob seemed oblivious to Susan's little improprieties.

One day Jenny was called out of town to assist an ailing relative. Upon returning home several days later, she walked into her kitchen only to find Susan preparing dinner for the family! Jenny was livid but said nothing to Susan. She politely thanked her for her efforts to help them out. Later that night, she confronted Bob about the entire situation. He was shocked that Jenny had entertained any negative thoughts about Susan's motives. He was certain that she was only trying to help, and he dismissed Jenny's suggestion that he have a talk with her. Consequently, Susan continued her unwise behavior.

Finally, Jenny decided the situation was taking too heavy a toll on her. She was beginning to resent Bob for minimizing her concern and felt deep anger toward Susan for her insensitivity and lack of wisdom. Jenny had kept quiet for "peace sake," but was far from experiencing inner peace. She knew what she had to do.

She phoned Susan at her office and asked if they could meet. When they met, the gist of the conversation went as follows:

Jenny: "Thank you, Susan, for taking time out of your lunch hour to see me."

Susan: "Oh, it's no problem. I'm always available to you and Pastor Bob."

Jenny: "I know, I know. In fact, that's what I want to talk to you about. I need you to help me to protect my husband's reputation. I'm sure you're not aware of it, but I've noticed several actions on your part that would cause me and others to look suspiciously at Bob. For instance [specific incidents noted]. In light of these, I thought I should speak to you about them."

Susan: "I am shocked [tears, tears] that you feel this way! I was just trying to be of service to you both. I won't even speak to him again if that makes you happy. I'm sorry that I ever extended myself at all [more tears]."

Jenny: "I didn't come down here to upset you. I just wanted you to know the effect your behavior was having on me and the potential impact on Bob's ministry. I hope that we can continue to maintain a relationship—one that honors God and that will be mutually rewarding. Do you mind if we pray together now?"

The story above is true, though the names have been changed. I applaud Jenny for her initiative and the calm and mature manner in which she conducted the confrontation. However, Bob should have handled the situation. Even though he is a pastor and a spiritual leader, his style is to avoid conflict. He is an Abdicator (see chapter 5). Notice that Jenny owned the issue. She didn't say, "Some of the members are talking." She didn't accuse. She simply explained how Susan's behavior was affecting her.

Use the Sandwich Approach

Conducting an effective confrontation is a lot like preparing a steak sandwich. A basic sandwich consists of bread, meat, and another piece of bread. The bread makes the eating of the sandwich more pleasurable. The steak is the "meat of the matter," the real issue of the confrontation.

The bread is a positive statement that lays the foundation for the confrontation. It affirms the person's worth and your commitment to the relationship. The statement should be true and not empty flattery. For instance, before Beth tells her husband that she needs more personal attention from him, she might say: "John, I really appreciate what a good provider you are. I never have to worry about the bills being paid. Your sense of responsibility gives me great comfort." Such affirmation will surely cause John to be more receptive to hear what is making his wife unhappy. She continues, "I need more affection from you..." Remember to refrain from saying *but* or *however* after the bread; these words act as giant erasers of what was just stated.

Sometimes the bread is more effective when put in the form of an open-ended question. Once we met one of Darnell's cousins, a woman from Georgia in her early twenties. When she visited our church, we noticed that she was exuberant and responsive to the pastor's message during the service. We went to lunch later and had a great time. When she told us she did not go to church regularly, I jokingly said, "If we had known that you were a heathen, we wouldn't have treated you to lunch." (Now understand that Darnell and I regularly use this term jokingly to refer to wayward Christians, and the conversation had been lighthearted all day.)

She was offended by the remark, but I admired how she dealt with it. About an hour later—okay, so she fumed a while—she asked me, "Deborah, what did you mean by the term *heathen*?" When I explained that we use it jokingly, she told me she thought it was offensive. I apologized and made a note to include the incident in this book. Notice that she got clarification of my intentions before drawing a conclusion.

In using the sandwich approach, it's important to include both pieces of bread. This allows you to close the confrontation positively. Express your commitment to work toward a positive relationship. The person should leave the confrontation knowing that you are rejecting his behavior and not him personally.

To reiterate, the opening bread and closing bread are an absolute must to make the meat of the matter more digestible. However, the offender will most likely fixate on the meat—or what they perceive as the negative aspect of the confrontation. Therefore, go heavy on the bread, but maintain sincerity.

Criticize Constructively

No one enjoys receiving or giving criticism. Like the words *diet* and *confrontation*, the word *criticism* has gotten a bad rap because of its association with negative situations. But the definition of criticism is "the act of making a judgment based on analysis and evaluation." To learn to receive and to give criticism like a pro, you must change your mind-set about the purpose of criticism.

I've learned that good, constructive criticism can provide me with information I can use to grow. Information is power. If I have information on how I am perceived or how my behavior is affecting those around me, I can more effectively achieve my personal and business goals.

Of course, the criticism must be constructive. Negative comments about a person's character or judgment do not build, but rather tear down. Never put another person down. When you make fun, belittle, or ridicule somebody, especially in front of others, you have just created an enemy. Always be careful to preserve the dignity of another person, Christian or non-Christian. Do unto others as you would have them do unto you.

Once I was at a client's office and witnessed an awful confrontation between two Christians of the opposite sex. She attacked his manhood; he attacked her womanhood. The rest of the staff was stunned and dismayed by their outburst. As a Christian, I was embarrassed. Satan had gotten a victory.

In any response to conflict, the focus must always be on the person's behavior, not his *personhood*, that is, his personality, judgment, or character. The more spiritually mature we are, the more able we are to separate a person from his behavior. God has set the example. He hates sin, but He loves the sinner. When Jesus confronted the woman caught in adultery, He told her that He did not condemn her. But He also admonished her to "go and sin no more" (John 8:11). He separated her sin from her personhood.

Don't be quick to make an accusation. Take time to get the facts. Listen with an open mind. The ability to see both sides of an issue can make you a great peacemaker and a trusted source for complete objectivity.

"What You Are Doing Is Not Good"
Jethro Versus Moses

The Israelites had finally escaped the clutches of the king of Egypt, but life was still no picnic—for them or for Moses their deliverer. Problems abounded.

> The next day Moses took his seat to serve as judge for the people, and they stood around him from morning till evening. When his father-in-law saw all that Moses was doing for the people, he said, "What is this you are doing for the people? Why do you alone sit as judge, while all these people stand around you from morning till evening?"

> Moses answered him, "Because the people come to me to seek God's will. Whenever they have a dispute, it is brought to me, and I decide between the parties and inform them of God's decrees and laws."

> Moses' father-in-law replied, "What you are doing is not good. You and these people who come to you will only wear yourselves out. The work is too heavy for you; you cannot handle it alone. Listen now to me and I will give you some advice, and may God be with you" (Exodus 18:13-19 NIV).

Here we have a glimpse of the administrative side of life in the wilderness. We see Moses in his new roles as interpreter of God's laws and conflict consultant, among other things. Moses was obviously a man of great patience and discipline to be able to sit all day and listen to the problems of the multitude. Thank God for the intervention of his father-in-law Jethro. We can learn the following lessons from Jethro's confrontation with Moses over his self-destructive behavior.

LESSON ONE: We can criticize with more ease when we have earned the right to do so.

Jethro was not just Moses' father-in-law; he was his former employer (Exodus 3:1) who willingly released Moses to return to Egypt to free the Israelites (Exodus 4:18). He had provided for Moses' family until the Israelites were safely in the wilderness, and then he had reunited them with Moses (Exodus 18:5). He had been sincerely glad for all of God's goodness to Israel. He was not envious that Moses had been exalted to such an honorable position as head of all Israel. He was not looking for ways to be critical. He cared about Moses and his welfare.

A close friend, who claims to be a Christian, told me he was at his wit's end with his rebellious 11-year-old daughter. Being familiar with his anger management problem, I asked him how he responds to her when she resists or disobeys him. He confessed that sometimes his actions bordered on physical abuse. I told him that he sounded out of control and needed to enter counseling right away along with his daughter.

"Well, maybe so. I'll see," he said.

I replied without hesitation, "Look, I'm going to find a therapist and make an appointment for you right away. That's that!"

I knew that I could be adamant with him because he knows beyond a shadow of a doubt that I have a genuine concern for his well-being.

LESSON TWO: Criticism is more effective when coupled with a specific suggestion or recommendation for improvement.

To tell someone, "What you are doing is not good," can be very frustrating to the person if he is doing all that he knows to do. Jethro gave Moses a concrete and workable recommendation. He also gave it in the right spirit, not as a mandate, but as an option for Moses to pray about and present to God.

"You must be the people's representative before God and bring their disputes to him. Teach them the decrees and laws, and show them the way to live and the duties they are to perform. But select capable men from all the people—men who fear God, trustworthy men who hate dishonest gain—and appoint them as officials over thousands, hundreds, fifties and tens. Have them serve as judges for the people at all times, but have them bring every difficult case to you; the simple cases they can decide themselves. That will make your load lighter, because they will share it with you. If you do this and God so commands, you will be able to stand the strain, and all these people will go home satisfied" (Exodus 18:19-23 NIV).

Notice that Jethro explained how the recommendation would benefit Moses as well as the multitude. This was no attempt to manipulate. Jethro had a genuine concern for Moses' well-being.

LESSON THREE: We must never become too big or too important to be teachable.

Moses readily accepted Jethro's advice even though Jethro didn't have the face-to-face relationship with God that Moses enjoyed. Moses did not allow pride to reign in his life. He was the meekest man on the face of the earth (Numbers 12:3).

Receiving Criticism

For some people, constructive criticism can be hard to receive because it forces them to acknowledge their fallibility. When we have established a reputation as a role model, a person of excellence, and someone people look to for knowledge and wisdom, it can be painful to face the fact that we may occasionally be wrong. We believe our own publicity; we buy into the image that others have of us. We enjoy that position on top of the pedestal. One of our greatest fears is the fear of falling off it. Trying to live up to that perfect image can be quite stressful and can cause us not to undertake endeavors that would reward and benefit others.

Several years ago, I had recurring dreams of being at or near the top of a high building and on the verge of falling. I'd often awaken with a sense of panic. After some introspection, I finally acknowledged that I had a fear of achieving great success; I feared that I would not be able to maintain it and would thus experience the humiliation of a great failure.

As hard as it may be to admit, many times you may find yourself trying to stay on the pedestal where well-meaning people have placed you. What a stressful place. You must make a decision to calmly step down and join the company of other excellence-seeking, fallible humans. The place on the pedestal belongs to God only.

Reject Destructive Criticism

If you are the person being confronted, it's important to remember that not all criticism is constructive and thus does not have to be accepted. Someone may desire to tear you down, diminish your self-esteem, or manipulate you into accepting his way of thinking. You must make it a habit to analyze the motive of a person who criticizes you. Ask yourself these thought-provoking questions:

- In the past, has this person demonstrated a genuine concern for my personal development?

- What does he have to gain personally if I implement the behavior he's recommending for me? What do I have to gain? What do I have to lose?

- Is his attitude one of helpfulness or am I feeling attacked or put down? Don't confuse a person's frustration with your behavior with an attack.

- After he criticizes me, do I feel like a hopeless failure, or does he express faith in my ability to change?

- Is he committed to sticking with me through the change?

If you conclude that a person is on a destructive criticism path, simply say, "Thank you for your input. I'll give it some thought." No need to verbalize your conclusion about her motives—unless her behavior becomes a pattern (it's important to confront negative patterns of behavior). "Well," you may ask, "what do I say to Ms. Negative?" A simple, unemotional response, such as "I'm open to specific recommendations that will help me," is your best option.

Admit Mistakes and Move Forward

King David provides a good model of how to move forward after a mistake. In 2 Samuel 12, Nathan the prophet confronted the king about the adultery he had committed with Bathsheba, the wife of Uriah, an officer in David's army. Bathsheba had conceived, and in his attempt to cover up his sin, David had her husband murdered in battle. Note his response when Nathan confronted him about his actions.

> Then David confessed to Nathan, "I have sinned against the LORD."
>
> Nathan replied, "Yes, but the LORD has forgiven you, and you won't die for this sin. Nevertheless, because you have shown utter contempt for the LORD by doing this, your child will die" (2 Samuel 12:13-14 NLT).

King David did not make excuses for his behavior. He could have blamed Bathsheba for tempting him by bathing where he could see her from the rooftop of his palace. He could have rationalized that he was overcome with the stress and pressures of being king. But no, he simply said, "I have sinned." The ability of anyone—the mighty or the lowly—to say "I was wrong" is a mark of maturity that will endear one to family, coworkers, or others much more than any attempt to make up for the wrongdoing. Furthermore, people who acknowledge their mistakes and forgive themselves are more apt to understand and forgive the mistakes of others. "Forgive us our debts, as we forgive our debtors" (Matthew 6:12).

King David did not allow his mistake or the child's death to immobilize him; he got on with the business of life. Notice his reaction when he was informed that the child had died:

> David replied, "I fasted and wept while the child was alive,
> for I said, 'Perhaps the LORD will be gracious to me and let
> the child live.' But why should I fast when he is dead? Can I
> bring him back again? I will go to him one day, but he cannot
> return to me" (2 Samuel 12:22-23 NLT).

David comforted his wife, Bathsheba. Shortly thereafter, she conceived another son, Solomon. He turned out to be the wisest man who ever lived. He was the product of a king who repented and went forward.

If you have a problem admitting your mistakes, I suggest you go right now and stand before a mirror and practice saying "I'm sorry. I was wrong." Resist the temptation to explain away or justify your actions. Experience a rise in your maturity gauge as well as a rise in others' respect for you.

I cannot conclude our discussion without a word to the perfectionists who whip themselves for every single mistake. Rather than using mistakes as learning tools for future development, they reject their entire being. "How could I be so stupid?" they ask. Christians are particularly vulnerable to this attitude. Yet, if I were to ask a group of God-fearing Christians, "How many of you have sinned in the last month?" most would acknowledge that they had. If I were to press further and ask, "How many consider yourselves sinners?" I would probably get no takers. After all, a sinner is someone who practices sin as a lifestyle, not someone who has committed his life to God but sins occasionally.

Well, why not apply the same thinking when it comes to our mistakes? Why color your, or anyone else's, entire character with a single mistake? Acknowledge it, ask forgiveness for it, learn from it, face the consequences of it with courage, and get on with life's next challenge. This is the ultimate demonstration of spiritual and emotional maturity.

Your Challenge

Using a currently unresolved conflict, prepare a "confrontation sandwich" that is sincere, direct, and unemotional.

Bread (affirmation): _____

Meat (the problem as it affects you): _____

Bread (affirmation): _____

10

Listening

Communication is the exchange of information. To effectively resolve interpersonal conflicts, we must accurately discern the root cause and be willing to listen objectively to the other person's input. This means hearing what is being said as well as what is not being said. The behaviors below are a few of the causes of the negative exchanges that can produce the cracks in our relationships. As you review the list, consider one of your recent conflicts and note which behavior from the list may have been the root cause.

- Fears/insecurity/jealousy
- Envy/greed
- Sin/rebellion
- Unexpressed or unmet expectations
- Unrealistic expectations
- Undefined roles and responsibilities
- Differing values, beliefs, philosophies, or opinions
- Competing desires
- Ineffective systems and processes
- Vain ambitions, power struggles

- Conflicting goals and objectives
- Violation of boundaries (expressed and unexpressed)
- Limited or scarce resources (time, money, space)
- Language barriers
- Lack of information
- Lack of understanding of the needs of different temperaments
- Poor relational skills

We need not only the skills and courage to say the right words in resolving conflict, we also must be skilled in listening. Again, I claim the words spoken of the Messiah as my goal:

> "The Lord GOD has given Me
> The tongue of the learned,
> That I should know how to speak
> A word in season to him who is weary.
> He awakens Me morning by morning,
> He awakens My ear
> To hear as the learned."
>   (Isaiah 50:4)

This is crucial to conducting an effective confrontation. By listening, we create a context or environment where people feel they have been heard and their thoughts or feelings have been validated. This is half the battle in resolving any conflict. Perhaps this is why we are admonished to be "swift to hear" (James 1:19). Listening is not a passive activity. It requires significant effort to discern what is really being said and even unsaid.

By listening, we create a context or environment
where people feel they have been heard and
their thoughts or feelings have been validated.

Several years ago, my husband and I belonged to a 16,000-member church that was in dire need of additional seating for its Sunday worship services. We had to do some skillful maneuvering to get a good seat near the front of the sanctuary. One Sunday, Darnell waited while I ducked into the lady's room prior to the start of the service. While refreshing my makeup, I got carried away in a conversation with another woman I'd never met. I was enjoying our fellowship so much that I lost track of the time. When I came outside, my normally patient husband was upset. He expressed his frustration that I had taken so long and reminded me that we had now forfeited our position near the front of the line to get into church. Well, I immediately felt perturbed with him for being perturbed with me.

Before I could respond negatively, the Holy Spirit prompted me to ask myself, "What is causing his frustration?" After all, he didn't have a preference for where we sat. I was the one who insisted on sitting near the front. Then it hit me—I had frustrated his attempt to please me. When I asked him later if this were so, he said yes. He gets a great thrill out of pleasing me, and, of course, I always express my pleasure with his efforts. I apologized for my insensitivity and silently reminded myself to make every effort to discern what is not being said.

"An Opportunity to Explain"
God Versus Adam and Eve

In our quest to "hear as the learned," we must discipline ourselves to listen rather than formulate a response to what is being said. Even if we think we already know all the facts of an issue, it pays to ask for and listen to an explanation. Notice the approach God used when He confronted Adam and Eve after they had eaten the forbidden fruit. He asked a series of questions and gave them an opportunity to explain their behavior before He pronounced judgment on them.

> Then the LORD God called to Adam and said to him, "Where are you?" [Question 1]

> So he said, "I heard Your voice in the garden, and I was afraid because I was naked; and I hid myself."

And He said, "Who told you that you were naked? [Question 2] Have you eaten from the tree of which I commanded you that you should not eat?" [Question 3]

Then the man said, "The woman whom You gave to be with me, she gave me of the tree, and I ate."

And the LORD God said to the woman, "What is this you have done?" [Question 4] (Genesis 3:9-13).

Of course, God already knew the answer to each of the questions He asked. But even He, in His mercy and long-suffering, waited and listened to their feeble excuses before banishing them from the Garden of Eden. Sincere questioning will often provide insight as to why a person resorted to his behavior. It also shows an earnest effort to understand his actions. Let's look at a similar example from the New Testament.

"Is It True?"
Peter Versus Ananias and Sapphira

The principle of asking before accusing or passing judgment is also demonstrated in the story of Ananias and Sapphira. The spirit of generosity abounded in the early church. People were selling their property left and right and bringing the proceeds to the church to distribute to those in need. Such unselfishness was a noble and godly act.

But there was a certain man named Ananias who, with his wife, Sapphira, sold some property. He brought part of the money to the apostles, claiming it was the full amount. With his wife's consent, he kept the rest.

Then Peter said, "Ananias, why have you let Satan fill your heart? You lied to the Holy Spirit, and you kept some of the money for yourself. The property was yours to sell or not sell, as you wished. And after selling it, the money was also yours to give away. How could you do a thing like this? You weren't lying to us but to God!"

> As soon as Ananias heard these words, he fell to the floor and died. Everyone who heard about it was terrified. Then some young men got up, wrapped him in a sheet, and took him out and buried him (Acts 5:1-6 NLT).

Peter first questioned Ananias about his motive for lying about the price he received for the land he had sold. Of course, Ananias never had a chance to answer him because he fell down and died. Only God knows what made him and his wife skim their own profits and pretend they had donated the entire proceeds. The lie had cost him his life. However, Peter did not assume that Sapphira was guilty also. He gave her the benefit of the doubt.

> About three hours later his wife came in, not knowing what had happened. Peter asked her, "Was this the price you and your husband received for your land?"
>
> "Yes," she replied, "that was the price."
>
> And Peter said, "How could the two of you even think of conspiring to test the Spirit of the Lord like this? The young men who buried your husband are just outside the door, and they will carry you out, too."
>
> Instantly, she fell to the floor and died. When the young men came in and saw that she was dead, they carried her out and buried her beside her husband. Great fear gripped the entire church and everyone else who heard what had happened (Acts 5:7-10 NLT).

Dear friends, let's challenge ourselves to listen carefully and to hear with discernment what others are saying—and not saying—about the root cause of our conflict with them.

"The Danger in Making Assumptions"
Israel Versus Israel

The Israelites had conquered their enemies in the Promised Land

and now it was time to settle into everyday life. Moses had allowed the Reubenites, the Gadites, and the half-tribe of Manasseh ("easterners") to inherit the land east of the Jordan River while the other nine and a half tribes ("westerners") settled on the west side. All twelve tribes had diligently fought their common enemies. Each had stood as one with their brothers to conquer the territory on both sides of the Jordan. Now the battles were over.

Joshua demobilized the army and dismissed the easterners to return to their families. Since the Jordan River would physically separate them from the western tribes and the center of worship, the easterners feared that someday the descendants of the westerners would say the easterners had no part in the worship of the God of Israel. Therefore, before the eastern soldiers crossed over to return to their families, they built a large altar near the Jordan River to commemorate their involvement in conquering the land. Big mistake!

The westerners heard about the altar and prepared to go to war against their brothers. Rather than approaching them with a desire to understand their actions, the westerners launched into a litany of accusations:

> When they arrived in the land of Gilead, they said to the tribes of Reuben, Gad, and the half-tribe of Manasseh, "The whole community of the LORD demands to know why you are betraying the God of Israel. How could you turn away from the LORD and build an altar for yourselves in rebellion against him? Was our sin at Peor not enough? To this day we are not fully cleansed of it, even after the plague that struck the entire community of the LORD. And yet today you are turning away from following the LORD. If you rebel against the LORD today, he will be angry with all of us tomorrow" (Joshua 22:15-18 NLT).

Isn't it frustrating when someone goes on and on with an accusation, and he's completely wrong? Before you're tempted to throw up your hands in frustration or interrupt with your explanation, discipline yourself to keep quiet until the barrage is over. Then respond in a calm manner as these leaders did:

> "The truth is, we have built this altar because we fear that in the future your descendants will say to ours, 'What right do you have to worship the LORD, the God of Israel? The LORD has placed the Jordan River as a barrier between our people and you people of Reuben and Gad. You have no claim to the LORD.' So your descendants may prevent our descendants from worshiping the LORD.

> "So we decided to build the altar, not for burnt offerings or sacrifices, but as a memorial. It will remind our descendants and your descendants that we, too, have the right to worship the LORD at his sanctuary with our burnt offerings, sacrifices, and peace offerings. Then your descendants will not be able to say to ours, 'You have no claim to the LORD'" (Joshua 22:24-27 NLT).

This example teaches us several lessons about averting, minimizing, or managing a conflict.

LESSON ONE: We should never make a decision or initiate an action that involves the affairs or the possessions of others without first consulting them.

We cannot assume that because our intentions are noble or innocent, or because the cause is worthy, everybody will understand or be happy with our actions.

I have had people, usually relatives, volunteer my time, talents, and even my home to others without any prior discussion with me or my husband. Obviously, this was before I learned to set boundaries in my life. If we are to live in harmony with others, we must respect their boundaries. Remember, people do not judge our *intentions*; they judge our *actions*.

LESSON TWO: When we feel that our boundaries have been violated, we should not conclude that the offender had less than honorable motives.

We should not prepare for war before we fully understand the other person's intentions or objectives. The westerners sent a delegation to the easterners, not to understand why the altar was erected, but to go to war against them. They assumed that the easterners were going to offer sacrifices on the altar. Such action would have been in direct violation of the law, which required everyone to sacrifice at the tabernacle, which at that time was at Shiloh. The westerners thought, "Why, these eastern rebels will bring down the wrath of God on all Israel."

It's amazing how quickly some choose to believe the worst about others—no matter what problems or experiences they may have been through together. They can simply hear that someone made a negative comment about them, and they prepare to fight. What a sad commentary on their spiritual and emotional maturity.

Lesson Three: We must always verify the facts or the truth of the matter before we make accusations.

The westerners accused the easterners of wrongdoing and reminded them of times past when Israel had offended God. The easterners proceeded to explain their reasons for building the altar. They simply wanted a memorial that would attest to their right to be involved west of the Jordan. Of course, if they had discussed the idea before their zealous act, the conflict would never have arisen.

Fortunately, this story has a happy ending. After the justification was given, an understanding was achieved. To the credit of the western delegation, they listened to and accepted the explanation. Even though they had come to fight, they took time to hear the other side. "When Phinehas the priest and the leaders of the community—the heads of the clans of Israel—heard this from the tribes of Reuben, Gad, and the half-tribe of Manasseh, they were satisfied" (Joshua 22:30 NLT).

War was averted.

LESSON FOUR: When we are the perpetrator of questionable actions, we must be quick to provide an explanation.

The easterners were appalled that their motives were misunderstood.

> "The LORD, the Mighty One, is God! The LORD, the Mighty One, is God! He knows the truth, and may Israel know it, too! We have not built the altar in treacherous rebellion against the LORD. If we have done so, do not spare our lives this day. If we have built an altar for ourselves to turn away from the LORD or to offer burnt offerings or grain offerings or peace offerings, may the LORD himself punish us" (Joshua 22:22-23 NLT).

It is not enough that God knows. Yes, our record may be written in heaven, but we live on earth among men. People deserve an explanation and an apology when we offend them. Jesus admonished us all, "Therefore if you bring your gift to the altar, and there remember that your brother has something against you, leave your gift there before the altar, and go your way. First be reconciled to your brother, and then come and offer your gift" (Matthew 5:23-24).

Your Challenge

The next time you attempt to resolve a conflict with someone, challenge your listening skills by waiting five complete seconds after the person finishes his statement before you respond. Put yourself in his shoes. Fully absorb all that he has said. Ask clarifying questions. Then calmly state your understanding of what the person has said. You will find that your listening will be rewarded.

11

Negotiating Future Behavior

Agreeing on future behavior is the final hurdle that people in conflict must overcome. After all, the whole purpose of the encounter is to resolve and bring closure to a problem. Even if the person who is confronted does not accept responsibility for his role in the conflict, it is important that you *both* agree on what each of you will do if a similar situation arises in the future. It may require mutual compromise. Someone may have to stop doing something; someone may have to start doing something. Whatever the decision, it should be win-win.

Even the daughters of Zelophehad (discussed in an earlier chapter) had to compromise. They had received the land allocation they had petitioned for—but they were required to marry men only from their tribe so that their uncles' concerns would be satisfied. A win-win settlement should always be the goal where possible. Agreement is particularly important when the behavior of one person or group will affect many others.

In a work environment, each person's performance has an impact on company goals; therefore, issues need to be resolved satisfactorily or plans set in place to resolve them in the future. For example, if you've asked for a promotion or a raise and the company has informed you that it won't be forthcoming, you and your supervisor should agree on what you need to do to improve your chances of getting what you want. A specific time should be set to review the situation. You may have to remind your supervisor that the time has come for the review, but this is no time to be shy or to fear that a reminder will be negatively received. Anyone who desires to become adept at resolving conflict must be proactive.

> Emotions and rational thinking work very much like a seesaw; when one side is high, the other is low.

A Word about Emotions

Confrontations often drive people to become highly emotional. Know that the silence, tears, anger, or other emotional behavior will prevent you from having a rational discussion and resolution of the problem. Emotions and rational thinking work very much like a seesaw. When emotions are high, rational thinking will be low. And if you employ only rational, objective thinking without concern for the person's emotions and feelings, the issue will not be resolved to everyone's satisfaction. The emotions must be acknowledged and worked through; ignoring them will only make matters worse. When you acknowledge people's emotions, you let them know that you value them and their feelings. Here are some ways to let people who are upset know that you are aware of their feelings:

- "Mary, you seem pretty upset. I can see that our decision to close the school is really affecting you."

- "Bob, your silence concerns me. When you refuse to give me any feedback, I'm at a loss as to how I can address your concern."

- "Betty, I can see from your tears that this is a very emotional subject for you. Would it be better if we met about this later?"

The important thing is to remain calm and refrain from minimizing the person's feelings. The expression of an emotion may be a useful clue that something is affecting a person in a way that could be causing the problematic behavior that is the focus of the confrontation.

If you know ahead of time that a person is prone to becoming emotional, don't shy away from confronting her simply to avoid the unpleasantness of the experience. As I mentioned in an earlier chapter, the ability to conduct an effective confrontation is a skill that is learned and perfected through practice and patience.

Once the emotions have been dealt with, you are now ready to negotiate an agreement about future behavior.

"Agreeing to Disagree"
Paul and Barnabas

Paul and Barnabas were a great team. Both apostles had a passion for God. Through their anointed preaching, an untold number of souls in many cities had received salvation. They had performed many miracles, resolved church conflicts, and experienced the trials and triumphs of ministry. On their first missionary tour, Barnabas' relative, a young man by the name of John Mark, had joined them. However, he had grown homesick and returned to Jerusalem. Now it was time for the dynamic duo to embark upon their second tour.

> Then after some days Paul said to Barnabas, "Let us now go back and visit our brethren in every city where we have preached the word of the Lord, and see how they are doing." Now Barnabas was determined to take with them John called Mark. But Paul insisted that they should not take with them the one who had departed from them in Pamphylia, and had not gone with them to the work. Then the contention became so sharp that they parted from one another. And so Barnabas took Mark and sailed to Cyprus; but Paul chose Silas and departed, being commended by the brethren to the grace of God (Acts 15:36-40).

Here is a situation where two spiritual giants couldn't resolve their conflict. Their individual perspective on the problem highlights the difference in their temperaments. Paul, the decisive, no-nonsense, focused apostle was unwilling to take John Mark on another evangelistic tour. Paul must have reasoned that they were on a mission from God and had no time for flakes.

True to the meaning of his name ("son of encouragement"), Barnabas, the understanding, long-suffering, and loving apostle, was not the type to strike anybody's name off his list because of a single failure. It was he who had brought Paul, after his conversion to Christ, to the skeptical disciples. He had vouched for Paul's credibility and convinced them to accept him (Acts 9:27). He could not turn his back on anyone, especially a relative. After all, charity begins at home. And now he found himself at odds with the man he had shared so many spiritual experiences with. Only one of them could be right regarding the decision whether to give John Mark another chance. Who was out of step with God on this one, Paul or Barnabas?

In reading this story, I am reminded of an incident that happened during my junior year in high school. I was determined to be a part of an elite group of majorettes who led the band onto the football field for the half-time show. Now, physical coordination has never been my strong suit—but perseverance is. During the initial rehearsals, I had a difficult time keeping my line of musicians marching in a straight line. They were following me! When the line would veer to the right, Mr. Jones, our band leader, would yell like a drill sergeant, "Smith, straighten that line!" I'd do fine for a few minutes, and then I'd veer to the left. "Smith, straighten that line!" Finally, in desperation, Mr. Jones gave me some advice that solved the problem. In my attempt to keep in step, I had been focusing on the majorettes on either side of me. He advised, "Keep your eyes on the drum major. Everybody who is in step with the drum major will be in step with each other!"

What a powerful principle. I have applied this advice to my marriage and to numerous conflict situations, especially with Christians. Everybody who is in step with God, who should be the Drum Major of our lives, will be in step with each other. Since you have no control over anybody else's relationship with God, your objective must be to make sure that you are in right relationship with Him. Ask Him, "Am I out of step with You on this issue?" Listen for His answer.

Well, back to Paul and Barnabas. Neither was willing to concede to the other, so they parted ways. Here are a few of the conflict management lessons we can learn from their clash:

LESSON ONE: No matter how spiritual a person is, everyone is subject to a blind spot when it comes to a relative.

I have seen the most anointed ministers suffer long—too long—with a family member in a leadership or other critical position, to the detriment of the entire ministry. (This was not necessarily the case with Barnabas (see Lesson Five below).) Rare is the leader who has the objectivity to look beyond that blood bond and focus on what is best for the organization. Equally rare is the church board of directors with the courage to insist that a change be made. Most boards will take an Accommodator approach and let the minister "have it his way." The kingdom of God often suffers for it.

LESSON TWO: We must actively work toward a mutually acceptable resolution.

When we fully grasp the truth that *agreement* is the place of power, we will be more willing to yield our druthers and preferences so that unity is achieved. Neither Paul nor Barnabas proposed an alternate solution (perhaps another young man to assist them). Both dug in their heels. Both took the "My Way" approach. Paul's stance: "I won't allow him to go." Barnabas' position: "I won't go without him."

LESSON THREE: We must be willing to seek the help of a third party when we cannot resolve the problem. While Jesus laid out the procedures to be followed when someone sins against us, I have found the same approach to be helpful when I have come to an impasse in my one-on-one effort to settle a matter:

"If another believer sins against you, go privately and point out the offense. If the other person listens and confesses it, you have won that person back. But if you are unsuccessful, take one or two others with you and go back again, so that everything you say may be confirmed by two or three witnesses. If the person still refuses to listen, take your case to the church. Then if he or she won't accept the church's decision, treat that person as a pagan or a corrupt tax collector" (Matthew 18:15-18 NLT).

The next step was for Paul and Barnabas to seek the help of other church members. But it appears that no such input was sought. The church simply stood on the sidelines and let them battle it out. Even though a conflict may be between only two individuals, those of us who see our brothers and sisters at odds need to consider our role as peacemakers. "Blessed are the peacemakers: for they shall be called the children of God" (Matthew 5:9 KJV). Peacemakers are people who actively seek to make peace. They initiate the effort to achieve unity.

To be a peacemaker involves risk. It is not a task for the fainthearted or the spiritually immature. Objectivity and confidentiality must be maintained as we attempt to get each party to come to agreement.

LESSON FOUR: Sometimes the best resolution of a conflict is a separation, even if it is temporary.

Now, don't run out and divorce your spouse. I am simply saying that many times the parties to a conflict are too emotionally attached to the issue and need space to rethink their stance. God can use separation for His glory. Because Paul and Barnabas parted, the gospel was preached in even more cities.

Should you decide that a temporary separation is the best option in your situation, try to come to agreement on how long it will be. In some friendships, one party may have outgrown the relationship. I don't think it's always necessary to acknowledge the end of a relationship. Some people may be too emotionally damaged by what they perceive as rejection. In that case, wisdom would dictate a phase out instead. Being unavailable for most activities will usually convey the message. Of course, I'm a proponent of the direct approach in most situations. However, we must be careful to consider a person's psychological and spiritual state and to deal with them accordingly.

LESSON FIVE: When we determine that we have been wrong, we need to admit it.

Often our erroneous assessments and assumptions cause conflict. In the case of Paul and Barnabas, Paul realized near the end of his life that John Mark really wasn't a flake. He wrote from prison to Timothy asking him to bring Mark to him. "Only Luke is with me. Get Mark and bring him with you, for he is useful to me for ministry" (2 Timothy 4:11).

The ability to say, "I was wrong," is a real challenge for a Dictator type like Paul. But here he provides a shining example. Have you ever been wrong about someone and told him so later? I've had a few people confess to me that they had pegged me to be one way and later found out they were wrong. I admired their courage to admit it. Of course, I question the good judgment of some of the confessions. One lady told me, "I assumed that you were stuck up, but I found out you're really down-to-earth!" (What is one to do with such revealing information?)

Let's be careful to use wisdom in how much "honest" information we reveal. The Bible says that "Everything is permissible for me—but not everything is beneficial" (1 Corinthians 6:12 NIV).

LESSON SIX: We must stay focused even when others don't take our side.

Acts 15:40 states that the Christians in Antioch gave Paul and Silas their blessing as they headed out on their mission. There is no mention of them offering any support for Barnabas and Mark (though they may have). If not, Barnabas was not deterred by this. I've seen ministers criticize and even ostracize other ministers over church hierarchy and power struggles. To Paul and Barnabas' credit, we never read that either made negative comments about the other after the split. Both focused on their respective missions and brought glory to God.

Your Challenge

The only behavior you have the power to change is your own. When considering a current conflict you may be experiencing, determine how much you are willing to compromise—without violating your core values or self-respect—to achieve harmony. Remember that both parties must agree with the final decision on how to go forward. Don't just keep quiet for peace sake.

12

Releasing the Offender

Volumes have been written on the importance of forgiveness. Yes, we know that if we don't forgive others, God won't forgive us. We know that unforgiveness can lead to physical and emotional problems. We know, we know, we know. But how do we conquer unforgiveness? This is the final step in resolving conflict. It is the step that allows both parties to move away from the conflict and on with their destiny.

I have learned some important lessons over the years as I've been faced with the need to forgive. Unforgiveness has had a stronghold in my family for years. I've seen some key members suffer mentally and emotionally for failure to release those who have offended or hurt them. I explained to my husband early in our marriage that it was a generational issue, and that it was going to stop with me. I would conquer unforgiveness.

I wish I could say making that decision made it easy. Every offense has sent me back to the feet of Jesus asking for help to conquer this emotional giant.

I was wrestling with a major hurt recently and really wanted to get past it and to forgive the offending party. I found that simply telling myself that I would forgive didn't stop the barrage of negative thoughts. I found myself continuing to rehearse the conversation that had led to the hurt. I really wanted to maintain a close relationship with the offender, but I couldn't get beyond the emotional wound. Then, like a flashlight in a dark tunnel, Philippians 2:13 exposed the heart of this dilemma: "For God is working in you, giving you the desire and the power to do what pleases him" (NLT).

> Forgiveness is not a natural response to a hurt or an offense; forgiveness requires supernatural intervention.

That's it! Forgiveness is not a *natural* response to a hurt or an offense; forgiveness requires *supernatural* intervention. My *natural* tendency was to see the person who had hurt me experience some pain too. But my spirit desired to do what would please God. I was trying too hard in my own strength to overcome the hurt. I just needed to let go and let God.

"Father," I prayed, "I thank You that Your Holy Spirit is already at work in me to give me the will to forgive. I delight in knowing that You don't leave a job half done. I receive Your power now to complete the work of forgiveness. I release all desire to avenge this wrong. You saw this situation before it happened, and in Your infinite wisdom, You allowed it to be so. I trust Your Word in Romans 8:28 that assures me that all things work together for my good because I love You and am called according to Your purpose. From this moment on, with the help of the Holy Spirit, I will not dwell on the situation but will declare Your Word instead. In Jesus' name, I pray. Amen."

I felt an immediate release from the bondage of unforgiveness.

I once heard someone say, "Forgiveness is a decision to set a prisoner free and then a discovery that the prisoner was you." If you already have a *desire* to forgive someone who has offended you, get excited; the Holy Spirit has already done half the job. Know that when He begins a good work, He is faithful to complete it.

Resist Retaliation

One day I went to our local post office to mail a package. As usual, the line was quite long and moving very slowly. I joined the line behind a man who appeared to be in his early forties and who wore heavy makeup and was clad in women's slacks and shoes. I mentally noted that he was shorter than I.

(Before I continue, I need to explain that my heart goes out to homosexuals. I believe that at the root of their deviation is a dysfunctional relationship, usually with the father; childhood molestation; or some other work of Satan. Therefore, I am always pleasant toward them. When I am in their presence, I often pray for their deliverance from such bondage.)

Frustrated with the long line, the man started complaining loudly about the postal staff's inefficiency. He yelled that he wanted to see the manager.

"This is ridiculous!" he shouted. "Every time I come here the service is terrible!"

I started quietly agreeing with him, hoping that would calm him.

"Are you in line just to buy a stamp?" I asked, being the ever-ready rescuer. "If so, I have one if you need it."

"No," he replied hesitantly. "I need something else too."

After what seemed like an eternity, the manager appeared. The man tore into him, attacking his qualifications for the job.

"Can't you control your staff?" he screamed. "You only have two people working the windows while everybody else is on break. You need to go back to school and learn how to manage!"

The manager did not respond to him directly. He simply began at the front of the line and attempted to determine those customers who needed only stamps versus those who needed other services. As he got closer to us, Mr. Confused's remarks grew meaner. Uncertain of what he might do next, I decided I should do something to calm him.

"Well, you've done a good job of getting his attention," I whispered to him. "Let's just give him space now and see what he does." As I said this, I touched him lightly on his shoulder. Big mistake!

"Don't put your hands on me!" he yelled. Then he said more calmly, "I know you don't mean any harm, but don't put your hands on me."

Words cannot describe the humiliation and embarrassment I felt. All eyes seemed focused on me. Here I was trying to spare the manager public humiliation, and look what I get. I resisted the urge to call him the politically incorrect name for homosexuals. I also reminded myself that God wouldn't have been pleased had I done so.

I must respond in a godly manner, I said to myself. *After all, I teach others how to handle such situations.*

I remained silent as he continued to complain—albeit less loudly, praise God!

Finally, he turned to me and asked, "Do you still have that stamp?"

Because for many years I have researched and memorized Scriptures dealing with conflict, the Holy Spirit will usually bring one to my remembrance—if I'm listening. That day it was Proverbs 19:11 (NIV):

> A man's wisdom gives him patience;
>   it is to his glory to overlook an offense.

I decided to respond just as the Scripture commanded—well sort of. I looked right over his head in stony silence. He wasn't getting my stamp! *Humph! That'll teach him not to embarrass me!*

The problem with retaliation is that it feels good to the flesh, but it grieves your spirit—and God's. I realized that in a subtle, passive-aggressive way, I had attempted to avenge the wrong that had been done to me. I had failed a spiritual test. Satan had gotten the victory. All I could do was repent.

Now, this incident may seem like a small thing, but we must remember that it's "the little foxes that spoil the vines" (Song of Solomon 2:15). If we can resist the temptation to retaliate in little things, we will develop retaliation-resistant muscles that will help us to overlook larger offenses.

Let's look at a story of how a powerful man confronted an offense and found a way to continue a relationship with the offenders.

"No Fool Twice"
Jephthah Versus His Nonrepentant Brothers

Jephthah was born the illegitimate son of a man named Gilead. His mother was a harlot. He grew up in the household with Gilead's other legitimate sons who later chased him away. "You will not get any of our father's inheritance," they said, "for you are the son of a prostitute" (Judges 11:2 NLT). He moved to the land of Tob, followed by a band of rebels. He soon developed a reputation as a mighty warrior.

> At about this time, the Ammonites began their war against Israel. When the Ammonites attacked, the elders of Gilead sent for Jephthah in the land of Tob. The elders said, "Come and be our commander! Help us fight the Ammonites!"
>
> But Jephthah said to them, "Aren't you the ones who hated me and drove me from my father's house? Why do you come to me now when you're in trouble?"
>
> "Because we need you," the elders replied. "If you lead us in battle against the Ammonites, we will make you ruler over all the people of Gilead" (Judges 11:4-8 NLT).

There are so many confrontation and conflict-management lessons in this story that I'll try to contain myself and discuss only a few.

LESSON ONE: Rejection can be part of God's divine plan.

Jephthah was rejected for a reason completely outside of his control— he was illegitimate. When he was cast out by his half brothers, he accepted their rejection and moved on with his life.

Perhaps you've experienced the emotional devastation of rejection. You may have been rejected because you were old, young, intelligent, dumb, pretty, ugly, privileged, poor, attractive, unattractive, sophisticated, unsophisticated, male, female, white, black (or, in the opinion of some, too black). This list is endless. The crux of the matter is that you were different! What has helped me to cope with such rejection is the assurance of divine destiny. Through it all, God has a plan for my life. Every hurt, every rejection, and every disappointment has made me who I am today.

The rejection forced Jephthah to the land of Tob. Most likely, it was there that he learned and perfected the art of war. If he had been accepted by his brothers and stayed home with them, he would have been in the same helpless position as they were when the Ammonites came against the Gileadites. Notice that he never sought to do them harm for rejecting him.

Lesson Two: We do not have to be a fool twice.

Jephthah was not so emotionally needy that he jumped at the chance to be in relationship with those who had previously rejected him. Notice when they asked him to come and be their captain, they never said they were sorry for casting him out, nor that they'd had a change of heart and now wanted to embrace him. They simply needed a warrior to lead them in battle.

Not missing the motive, Jephthah responded in essence, "Wait a minute. We can't just go forward as if nothing has happened. Our relationship has been damaged. Sounds as if you just want to use me, since you're only coming to me because you're in distress. Let's get an understanding of the type of relationship we're going to have."

The first offer the leaders of the people of Gilead made to Jephthah was to be only the captain of their army even though they had previously agreed among themselves that whoever would lead them in battle would also be made the head of all Gilead (Judges 10:18). Once Jephthah boldly stated that he wanted to understand the relationship they now wanted, they sweetened the pot and offered him the headship of all Gilead (vv. 8,11).

I see a type of Jesus in Jephthah's dealings with these leaders of Gilead. Many of us want Jesus to be our Savior only, but as Jephthah wanted to be more than a captain, so Jesus wants more than to save us from eternal damnation. He wants to be our Lord! He wants to rule our lives.

This story lets us know that God does not require us to put ourselves in a position to be hurt twice. Many times when a trust has been breached, we need to forgive and exercise wisdom in how we go forward. There are people in my life I know not to share confidential information with; my interaction with them is limited to certain activities and surface conversations. However, I still love them and desire to be in relationship with them on some level.

Many of us put ourselves in the position to be hurt twice, like the man who went to the doctor for a severe burn on his right cheek.

"How did this happen?" the doctor asked.

"I was ironing and watching television when the phone rang. I picked up the iron instead of the phone."

"I see," the still puzzled doctor said. "But how did you get the burn on your left cheek.

"He called back!" the man exclaimed.

That's essentially what we do to ourselves when we allow someone to hurt us twice. Jephthah responded wisely to his brothers so that he would not be hurt by them again.

The *decision* to forgive should be immediate. No one has to earn our forgiveness. However, restoring trust is a process. Trust must be earned over time. The perpetrator of the offense must show the fruit of repentance—consistent behavior that gives evidence he has had a change of heart. Jesus said, "Prove by the way you live that you have repented of your sins and turned to God" (Matthew 3:8 NLT).

LESSON THREE: Man does not determine our destiny.

Even though his brothers proclaimed that Jephthah would never have an inheritance among the Gileadites, we find them begging him to come back when they faced a powerful enemy. The world has a saying that, "It's not over until the fat lady sings." Men may declare what you can't be or won't do until they are blue in the face, but God has the last word. "For I know the thoughts that I think toward you, saith the LORD, thoughts of peace, and not of evil, to give you an expected end" (Jeremiah 29:11 KJV).

LESSON FOUR: A unity walk requires unity talk.

Jephthah immediately embraced the new relationship. "Then Jephthah sent messengers to the Ammonite king with the question: 'What do you have against us that you have attacked our country?'" (Judges 11:12 NIV).

He referred to the land of the Gileadites as "our country." His history in Gilead had been marred by his rejection. That was all behind him now. He fully embraced the cause. He was ready to walk in unity. A unity walk required unity talk.

Have you ever noticed how some people refer to the activities of their church or organization as events "they" (rather than "we") are sponsoring? Or what about wives who refer to their children as "my son" or "my daughter" rather than "our child"? Are you one of these people? You'd be surprised at the impact unity talk will have on your attitude and relationships. You'll find yourself being less critical of others once you make such "team talk" a habit.

"Buying Forgiveness"
Jacob Versus Esau

Another dynamic in the saga of forgiveness is found in the story of Jacob and his twin brother, Esau, as recorded in Genesis 27. Rebekah, their scheming mother, conspired with Jacob, the younger of the two, to cheat Esau out of the birthright due him as the firstborn. Among many other benefits, the birthright included a special spiritual blessing by the father as well as a double portion of the inheritance. Because Jacob was Rebekah's favorite, she devised a plan to trick her ailing, sight-challenged husband, Isaac, into bestowing the blessing on Jacob.

God had already advised Rebekah during her pregnancy that the older son would serve the younger (Genesis 25:23)—in spite of the benefits inherent with their birth order. However, Rebekah was not content to let God bring His will to pass His way. She had to assist Him. Further, Esau had already sold his birthright to Jacob for a bowl of lentil stew during a fit of hunger (Genesis 25:33-34). Clearly, Jacob was destined to have the superior position in life.

When Esau learned that he had been tricked out of the blessing as a result of Jacob and Rebekah's scheme, he was furious. He wanted to kill his brother. Esau's response is not surprising when we consider the gravity of the situation; this would affect the rest of his life. He was hurt. Hurting people often hurt people.

Rebekah, demonstrating little understanding of human behavior, naively believed that the matter would blow over soon. She urged Jacob to flee to Haran to live temporarily with her brother Laban until Esau's fury subsided. She told him, "When your brother is no longer angry with you and forgets what you did to him, I'll send word for you to come back from there. Why should I lose both of you in one day?" (Genesis 27:41-45 NIV).

So Rebekah shipped Jacob off to Uncle Laban. But Jacob could not escape the law of sowing and reaping. Those who deceive will be deceived. In Haran, he worked seven years to marry Laban's youngest daughter only to be deceived into marrying the older daughter. When he confronted Laban about the deception, he was allowed to go ahead and marry the sister he loved, though it cost him seven additional years of labor. He was also subjected to numerous other deceptions. But he prospered anyway. After all, he had received the blessing.

After many years, the Lord told Jacob to go back home to the land of Canaan and that He would be with him there. Jacob, assuming that Esau was still upset with him, prepared a generous peace offering consisting of numerous cattle and other gifts. Jacob sent messengers to tell Esau that he was on the way and was bringing lots of presents for him. The messengers returned and advised Jacob that Esau and four hundred of his men were coming to meet him. They would arrive tomorrow. You can imagine the anxiety Jacob must have experienced. *Will he avenge the wrong that I perpetrated upon him? Will he receive me? What will he do?*

But Jacob found favor with God. That night he had an encounter with an angel who changed his name and his nature. His new name became Israel, and he was no longer a trickster! Then Esau arrived.

"And what were all the flocks and herds I met as I came?" Esau asked.

Jacob replied, "They are a gift, my lord, to ensure your friendship."

"My brother, I have plenty," Esau answered. "Keep what you have for yourself."

But Jacob insisted, "No, if I have found favor with you, please accept this gift from me. And what a relief to see your friendly smile. It is like seeing the face of God! Please take this gift I have brought you, for God has been very gracious to me. I have more than enough." And because Jacob insisted, Esau finally accepted the gift (Genesis 33:8-11 NLT).

Notice that Jacob never said, "I'm sorry that I stole your birthright and your blessing. Please forgive me." He offered no formal apology. He basically said, "I'd like to pay you for your forgiveness. Accept my gifts." Some offenders may never offer the apology that you want in the *manner* you desire. If reconciliation is your goal, then you'll have to do as Esau did and accept their indirect efforts as their apology—and stop wishing that things were different.

Many men will buy their wives a gift or do something extra nice rather than apologize for their bad behavior. Once, while conducting a marriage seminar, I asked the women to raise their hands if they would prefer an apology rather than a present. The majority of the hands went up. I then asked how many would prefer an apology *and* a present. It was unanimous!

I know two neighbors who experienced a major rift in their relationship when one of the neighbors offended the other's wife. The offending neighbor made several attempts to express his contrition, but to no avail.

"Hasn't he come over and asked for forgiveness?" I asked the offended neighbor in my effort to reconcile them.

"Oh yes, he has," he replied. "But he has not *apologized*. Therefore, I can't forgive him."

Here was someone who would be satisfied with hearing only certain words. As people of God, we must grow up and exercise some spiritual maturity. We can't control what others do; we can control only our response. Further, if we insist that someone apologize to us in a certain way, then we need to let them know specifically what we want.

Holding a grudge is like holding a hot coal; it will keep burning you until you let it go.

"Leaving Vengeance to God"
Joseph Versus His Repentant Brothers

I'm sure that everyone who has ever attended Sunday school knows the story of Joseph found in Genesis 37–50. Many lessons can be learned from his life of adversity (sold into slavery by his envious brothers and thrown into prison on a false accusation) and from his rise to prominence in Egypt after orchestrating a bailout plan that saved millions, including his brothers and their families, from starvation during a severe and protracted famine. Through it all, he maintained a great attitude and a commitment to high moral standards. Although he was reconciled to his brothers, after their father's death, they feared that Joseph would surely retaliate and do them harm.

> So they sent this message to Joseph: "Before your father died, he instructed us to say to you: 'Please forgive your brothers for the great wrong they did to you—for their sin in treating you so cruelly.' So we, the servants of the God of your father, beg you to forgive our sin." When Joseph received the message, he broke down and wept. Then his brothers came and threw themselves down before Joseph. "Look, we are your slaves!" they said.
>
> But Joseph replied, "Don't be afraid of me. Am I God, that I can punish you? You intended to harm me, but God intended it all for good. He brought me to this position so I could save the lives of many people. No, don't be afraid. I will continue to take care of you and your children." So he reassured them by speaking kindly to them (Genesis 50:16-20 NLT).

Joseph had long settled in his spirit that vengeance was God's job. In spite of all the inequities perpetrated against him, he never sought to avenge a wrong. From the time that he was sold away from his father at the tender age of 17 until he came into power in Egypt, he humbly submitted to divine providence. He believed, as we must, all things done *to* us or *against* us—even the intentional, evil deeds—will eventually work for our good. He had no intention of taking God's job by retaliating against his brothers.

For those who would dare to go to another level of spiritual maturity, it is not enough to refuse to retaliate; you must be willing to treat the offender like an enemy. Yes, that's right—like an enemy: "But I say to you, love your enemies, bless those who curse you, do good to those who hate you, and pray for those who spitefully use you and persecute you" (Matthew 5:44).

Are you willing to love, bless, do good to, and pray for those who have wronged you? Are you willing to be made willing?

One of my spiritual mentors was counseling me one day about forgiving a certain sister against whom I was harboring anger and resentment. She looked me in the eyes and said, "Deborah, you need to make her a focus of prayer. There is no way that you can harbor resentment against someone you are constantly interceding for and asking God to bless and prosper." She was right. Today, that sister and I are close friends.

Focusing on the Future

One morning I was speeding down the Pasadena freeway on my way to a workshop. I was so focused on getting there on time, I didn't notice the highway patrolman on the motorcycle behind me until he sounded his siren. When I pulled over, he approached my window and asked, "Don't you ever look back? I've been following you for quite some time." I explained that I was so preoccupied with getting to the workshop and with some other stress-inducing challenges that I didn't realize I was speeding. After my tearful plea for mercy, he admonished me to slow down and let me go without a citation. Thank you, Lord!

As I reflected on this incident later, the Lord began to speak to my heart about not looking back. Looking back can be a positive thing when our objective is to get useful information that will benefit the present. David took a *positive* look back before he slew Goliath.

> But David said to Saul, "Your servant used to keep his father's sheep, and when a lion or a bear came and took a lamb out of the flock, I went out after it and struck it, and delivered the lamb from its mouth; and when it arose against me, I caught it by its beard, and struck and killed it. Your servant has killed both lion and bear; and this uncircumcised Philistine will be like one of them, seeing he has defied the armies of the living God" (1 Samuel 17:34-36).

If you're going to look back, then you must be sure that your purpose is to rehearse a victory or to remember a lesson learned. Looking back should instill faith and courage to face the present.

On that freeway that morning, I could have looked back to see if it was safe to change lanes. But since I was already in the fast lane and had planned to stay there until the end of my journey, there was no need to look back. Looking back to bemoan the fact that I had just come through some unusually heavy traffic or to get another glimpse of the driver who had cut me off earlier would have impeded my progress or may have even caused me to crash into something in front of me.

A lot of people are constantly looking back instead of focusing on the future. They're not looking back to learn from what they've come through; they're just lamenting that whatever happened in the past happened. They ask, "Why me?" Before they know it, they have wrecked the future.

Let's take a lesson from the automakers. Haven't you noticed that your windshield is a lot larger than your rearview mirror? That's because you're supposed to spend more time looking forward than back! The apostle Paul, refusing to look back, proclaimed, "No, dear brothers and sisters, I have not achieved it, but I focus on this one thing: Forgetting the past and looking forward to what lies ahead, I press on to reach the end of the race and receive the heavenly prize for which God, through Christ Jesus, is calling us" (Philippians 3:13-14 NLT).

Remember Lot's wife? When God decided to destroy Sodom and Gomorrah for their wickedness, He sent angels to warn Lot and his family to get out of town. Their directives were very clear: "'Run for your lives!' the angels warned. 'Do not stop anywhere in the valley. And don't look back! Escape to the mountains, or you will die.' But Lot's wife looked back as she was following along behind him, and she became a pillar of salt" (Genesis 19:17,26 NLT).

Mrs. Lot disobeyed a direct angelic order; as a result, she became frozen in her "look back" stage. I'm sure all of us know at least one person whose conversation indicates that he or she is stuck in the past. The tragedy is that a lot of these people are Christians. No one enjoys their company. Most of their close relatives and friends look for ways to shorten their visits with them.

If you are one of these people, take heed now. Stop rehearsing the ills and inequities of the past. Ask God to help you focus on your future. You are not an eternal victim. Everything that has happened to you was permitted by God and will ultimately work for your good. Although you may never understand it all, believe the promise that God spoke through the prophet Jeremiah: "For I know the thoughts that I think toward you, says the LORD, thoughts of peace and not of evil, to give you a future and a hope" (Jeremiah 29:11).

If you are still alive—and obviously you are if you're reading this—you have not finished your assignment here on earth. You still have work to do. Focus on the future. Don't allow the past to dictate the quality of your life in the present or the future.

I am awed by the account of the three Hebrew boys, Shadrach, Meshach, and Abednego, whom King Nebuchadnezzar threw into the fiery furnace. When God delivered them out of the fire, "they didn't even smell of smoke!" (Daniel 3:27 NLT). There was no evidence, nothing that emanated from them, that indicated they had been in the fire.

I've encountered many people who "smell like smoke." Their attitude says, "I've been through the fire, and I'm upset with the world about it." They are the surly retail clerks, the insensitive nurses, the crabby ushers at church. What about you? Do you smell like smoke? Do you have a bad attitude that demonstrates you've been through the fire of affliction?

Some of us are bound by memories of the past. We rehearse the pain daily. Someone once told me a story about the circus elephant. A curious patron asked the elephant trainer how such a huge animal could be kept under control by being chained to a stake in the ground. Clearly he could pop the chain with little effort. "You don't understand," the trainer said. "When the elephant was quite young and unaware of his strength, he was bound with a chain that limited his mobility. He accepted this limitation as a permanent reality. So you see, it's not the *chain* that binds him, but his *memory!*"

If you are bound by debilitating memories, here's an antidote straight from the Word of God:

> O Lord our God, masters besides You
> Have had dominion over us;
> But by You only we make mention of Your name.
> They are dead, they will not live;
> They are deceased, they will not rise.
> Therefore You have punished and destroyed them,
> And made all their memory to perish.
>
> (Isaiah 26:13-14)

Whatever the haunting memory is, you must begin to declare your deliverance from its bondage. Even psychologists agree that when you speak forth positive words, you improve your mental health. The

Scottish philosopher, Thomas Carlyle, said that if you will proclaim your freedom from bondage, it will vanish.

During a dark period of my life, I held on to this passage until God turned my situation around. I marvel at the vast number of Christians who do not know how to use the Word of God to obtain their deliverance. His words have life; when you speak them, they are powerful. "For the word of God is living and powerful, and sharper than any two-edged sword, piercing even to the division of soul and spirit, and of joints and marrow, and is a discerner of the thoughts and intents of the heart" (Hebrews 4:12).

Your Challenge

You do not have to be trapped in the past, dwelling on offenses that have been done to you. Use these suggestions to get unstuck!

1. Put your tongue on a "no negativity" consecration for the next thirty days. After this period of time a habit should be established. Refuse to discuss any injustice or hurt from the past. Make yourself accountable to a close friend or relative. Please do not select anyone who has this same problem; negativity is contagious! And for goodness' sake, try to avoid those you normally commiserate with. If avoiding such a person is not possible, invite him or her to join you in your consecration. Replace every negative thought with a promise from God's Word. For more details on how to conduct this challenge, see my book, *30 Days to Taming Your Tongue* (Harvest House Publishers, 2005).

2. Begin to talk about and plan things you'd like to do. Start with a small project or activity and assign a due date to it. Goals without due dates are just wishes. Here are some suggestions to get you started:

   • plan a twenty to thirty minute walk with someone three days a week

- invite a few people over for a short prayer meeting or Sunday dinner within the next two weeks
- visit a hospice in the next few weeks

The possibilities are endless. You just need to get unstuck. Unlike Lot's wife, you still have the option of moving forward.

Forgiveness is simply releasing the desire to see the wrong avenged. Remember, holding on to a hurt or an offense is like holding a hot coal; the longer you hold it, the more it harms you. Let it go. You can do it with the help of the Holy Spirit, "for it is God who works in you both to will and to do for His good pleasure" (Philippians 2:13).

Finally, each time I am tempted to withhold forgiveness, I'm reminded that God wants me to be a *channel* of His grace and mercy and not a *reservoir*. Water flows *through* a channel but simply *accumulates* in a reservoir. God does not want us to accumulate forgiveness from Him for our sins but refuse to pass it on to others. He is forced to stop the flow. "But if you do not forgive men their trespasses, neither will your Father forgive your trespasses" (Matthew 6:15).

Part 4

Confrontation and
Personality Temperaments

13

The P.A.C.E.
Personality Profile

The major problems experienced by most organizations are not technology related; they are rooted in how people deal with each other. While every person is different, people are motivated by common fears and needs. Conflicts arise when these fears are tapped into or needs are unmet by others.

In Part 2 of this book, we looked at the four basic styles of managing conflict and confrontation. In this section, we will explore four basic temperaments that most of us reflect, not only in conflict, but also in our day-to-day interactions with others. These temperaments closely parallel how we choose to handle conflict.

> While every person is different, people are
> motivated by common fears and needs.

Hippocrates first introduced the concept of temperaments hundreds of years ago. He labeled them the Phlegmatic, the Sanguine, the Choleric, and the Melancholy. Since then, numerous variations have been put forth by various authors and mental health professionals. Most people find these descriptions intimidating and too difficult to remember. Not to worry. The P.A.C.E. Personality Profile discussed in the following pages will allow you to identify and remember the temperaments with ease. Each temperament is likened to the categories of people found on an airplane: Passenger, Attendant, Captain, and Engineer. Their descriptions parallel the Hippocrates model:

P-Passenger (Phlegmatic)
A-Attendant (Sanguine)
C-Captain (Choleric)
E-Engineer (Melancholy)

I interviewed several airline pilots in developing this profile, and they informed me that the position of flight engineer has been taken over by the computer, except on older planes. However, the Engineer function, even if carried out by a computer, describes the basic behavior of this temperament.

To get started, you need to determine your own temperament. As you become more familiar with the characteristics of each category, you will develop a better understanding of the temperament types and their needs and fears. And the better you understand the temperament of others, the better equipped you'll be to tailor your approach when confronting them.

Before you begin the test, decide the environment (work, home, social, church, or other) in which you wish to assess your normal behavior. This is important since many people tend to behave differently in different settings. When I took the test several years ago, it showed that my assertiveness was not as significant at home as it was at the office, where I had high-level financial and administrative responsibilities.

Follow the instructions carefully so that the results will accurately reflect your true nature.

P.A.C.E. Personality Temperament Quiz

Please note your Environmental Focus for this assessment:
  ☐ Work   ☐ Home   ☐ Social   ☐ Other

Instructions: Review all four lists of personality traits. Place a check by each trait that best describes your normal behavior in the chosen environment. Respond quickly and be honest. Please do not check the traits that you *desire* to possess, but only those you normally exhibit. When finished, total the number of checks in each category. The category with the highest number of checks is your dominant temperament; the next highest is your secondary temperament.

"P" TRAITS	"A" TRAITS
_____ Reserved	_____ Sociable, fun
_____ Likes routine	_____ Generous
_____ Contented	_____ Good at sales
_____ Tolerant	_____ Easily sold to
_____ Prefers to follow	_____ Inspires others
_____ Good listener	_____ Overcommits time
_____ Team player	_____ Hates routine
_____ Avoids conflict	_____ Good on stage
_____ Good under pressure	_____ Easily distracted
_____ Slow	_____ Spontaneous
_____ Low risk taker	_____ Compassionate
_____ Peaceful	_____ Encourager
_____ Diplomatic	_____ Optimistic
_____ Peacemaker	_____ Emotional
_____ Indecisive	_____ Seeks approval
_____ Dependable	_____ Often late
_____ Laid back	_____ Sensitive to others
_____ Patient	_____ Volunteers
_____ Likes status quo	_____ Persuasive
_____ Not generous	_____ Undisciplined
_____ Loyal	_____ Forgetful
_____ Timid	_____ Disorganized
_____ Unmotivated	_____ Likes recognition
_____ Reluctant	_____ Exaggerates
_____ Mumbles	_____ Not detailed
_____ **Total checks**	_____ **Total checks**

"C" TRAITS

____ Outspoken
____ Competitive
____ Usually right
____ Hates to apologize
____ Moves/Talks fast
____ Likes status symbols
____ Confronts interpersonal
      conflicts
____ Self-reliant
____ Confident
____ Resourceful, knowledgeable
____ Decisive
____ Productive
____ Strong-willed
____ Leader
____ Goal oriented
____ Controlling
____ Risk taker
____ Impatient
____ Unsympathetic
____ Intolerant
____ Direct, frank
____ Workaholic
____ Likes change
____ Often offends
____ Practical

____ **Total checks**

"E" TRAITS

____ Orderly
____ Neat
____ Enjoys technical work
____ Content in the
      background
____ Avoids confrontation
____ Complies with rules
____ Prone to depression
____ Serious
____ Faithful partner
____ Detailed
____ Analytical
____ Loyal
____ Disciplined
____ Worries
____ Buys top quality
____ Sensitive
____ Unforgiving
____ Few friends
____ Moody
____ Indecisive
____ Critical
____ Insecure
____ Appreciates music
____ Loves facts
____ Planner

____ **Total checks**

Scoring: Indicate the number of checks from each list:

P ____ A ____ C ____ E ____

What is your dominant temperament? ____

What is your secondary temperament? ____

In the next chapter, we will discuss the results of this assessment. I should caution that if you answered yes to a majority of the questions on more than two of the personality types, this could indicate that you are trying to be "all things to all men" (1 Corinthians 9:22), but not in the positive way the apostle Paul recommended for winning souls. You may be attempting to win friends or to meet the expectations of too many people (or you may be unclear about what others expect from you). Such behavior can cause a great deal of stress and lead to related illnesses.

Your Challenge

What aspects of your temperament have been the most problematic in your relationships (example: tendency to say yes when you want to say no, inflexibility, and so on)? What specific steps will you begin to take today to minimize or eliminate this behavior?

14

Understanding
the Temperaments

As you gain understanding of the various personality types, you will become skilled at capitalizing your strengths and recognizing the strengths that others bring to the table. You will also be aware of your weaknesses and learn to be more tolerant of the weaknesses of others. Let's look at the Passenger, Attendant, Captain, and Engineer temperaments in more depth.

The Passenger Temperament

Passengers participate passively in a flight. They do not get involved in the operation of the aircraft. They may have strong opinions about the flight, but in most instances, they do not confront the Captain. Passengers may even have questions, but they will either refrain from asking the flight attendant or will opt to ask another passenger.

Passengers usually do as they are told. They buckle their seat belts and return their seat backs to the full upright position for takeoff and landing. Passengers do not like change: no delays, no cancellations, no lost luggage, and please, no turbulence. They prefer the status quo; the flight should depart and arrive as scheduled. Everything should go smoothly.

The majority of the people on any flight are the passengers. The majority of people in life are Passengers. There are only a few Captains or leaders. This is all part of God's divine purpose. Imagine all chiefs and no Indians or all Indians and no chiefs. Would any purpose ever get accomplished?

Before we disdain Passengers, let's look at the strengths of this temperament. Passengers are good at reconciling conflicts between others because they believe so strongly in peace and harmony. Passengers are loyal and dependable. They are needed to accomplish goals and objectives. Without passengers, airlines could not remain in business. Factories and other businesses would have no one to perform the routine, day-to-day operations. Passengers prefer routine. They are the backbone of organized labor. Passengers are team players. In a crisis, they are capable of coming through. How many acts of passenger heroism have we read about when a plane has crashed or been hijacked?

Of course, the Passenger temperament has its weaknesses. Passengers prefer to maintain the status quo. Their greatest fear is the loss of security. They are the primary focus of all political campaigns since they represent the masses. Politicians promise security and stability, and Passengers buy the promise. When Passengers feel betrayed, they get even by quietly voting to "throw the bums out."

We see the Passenger temperament in action with the Israelites after the exodus from Egypt. On several occasions they reminded Moses that he should have maintained the status quo. The first time was when they felt trapped between Pharaoh's pursuing army and the Red Sea:

> As Pharaoh approached, the Israelites looked up, and there were the Egyptians, marching after them. They were terrified and cried out to the LORD. They said to Moses, "Was it because there were no graves in Egypt that you brought us to the desert to die? What have you done to us by bringing us out of Egypt? Didn't we say to you in Egypt, 'Leave us alone; let us serve the Egyptians'? It would have been better for us to serve the Egyptians than to die in the desert!" (Exodus 14:10-12 NIV).

The people would remind Moses on several other occasions that he should have just let things be. Passengers will not normally volunteer for leadership. They'll murmur that somebody should do something, but they are unlikely to step up to the plate unless forced by circumstances to do so. On another occasion, when the Israelites received the report that there were giants in the Promised Land, they complained,

> So all the congregation lifted up their voices and cried, and the people wept that night. And all the children of Israel complained against Moses and Aaron, and the whole congregation said to them, "If only we had died in the land of Egypt! Or if only we had died in this wilderness! Why has the LORD brought us to this land to fall by the sword, that our wives and children should become victims? Would it not be better for us to return to Egypt?" So they said to one another, "Let us select a leader and return to Egypt" (Numbers 14:3-4).

Passengers often cause Captains (whom we will discuss later) to assume their role by default. As a confessed Captain, I have often tried to resist taking the lead to allow others to do so—often to no avail. Passengers like to be led. They are generally not self-motivated; they must be wound up and put on the track if they are to get going.

Passengers are more relationship-oriented than task-oriented. Thus, they hate confrontation. In a conflict, Passengers may take the Abdicator approach. They will often retreat, emotionally rather than physically. After all, Passengers do not like change. They will stay in a relationship longer than any other personality group, just to maintain the status quo.

In a personal conflict with a Passenger, you must be on guard not to push too hard. You must express sincere appreciation for whatever the Passenger has accomplished. The sandwich approach discussed earlier is a must. Remember: Bread (appreciation), then Meat (the problem), and more Bread (appreciation).

Even though a Passenger may believe that you care about him, he still may not respond as quickly as you desire—especially if you are a Captain. You must be careful not to judge the Passenger as a passive, apathetic low achiever. He is steady, loyal, and will get the job done.

The Attendant Temperament

Flight attendants are primarily concerned with the comfort and safety of the passengers. They greet each passenger at the entrance to the plane and create a friendly atmosphere. They make conversation with complete strangers. Attendants show interest in whatever the stranger wants to discuss. They make every effort to satisfy the needs of passengers. In an emergency, the flight attendant is the first to move into action on behalf of the passengers. Each attendant is supposed to make every effort to leave a good impression on the passengers so they will continue to patronize that airline. Attendants are always volunteering: "Would you like something to drink?" "Blankets, anyone?" Sometimes they forget to bring the extra pillow or blanket that one passenger has requested because they are so busy accommodating another.

Attendants tend to overcommit themselves. My husband and I have a friend who stays in trouble with his wife because he is always rescuing someone in distress. He forgets that he has promised to be home at a certain time for a planned activity. He sincerely enjoys helping others, and everyone loves him. However, his wife doesn't always appreciate his self-sacrificing ways.

In managing conflict, the Attendant will normally take the Accommodator approach. In an earlier chapter, we saw Peter straddle the fence in his attempt to befriend Gentiles and Jews. Captain Paul, knowing what was best, confronted him about his hypocrisy (Galatians 2:11-15). Aaron chose to accommodate the wishes of the Israelites in the wilderness and built a golden calf (Exodus 32:4). Certain Jewish leaders chose not to openly acknowledge their faith in Jesus as the Messiah because they were afraid they would be ostracized by their peers (John 12:42). All of these Attendant personalities share a common thread: they feared rejection or the loss of social approval.

The other personality styles often view those with the Attendant temperament as flighty, superficial, and desiring the spotlight, since they are so good with people and are comfortable center stage. Remember that our opinions are not facts. We must accept the Attendant the way that God has made him.

Because the Attendant's greatest fear is rejection or the loss of social approval, those who confront the Attendant should be careful to let the Attendant know that only his behavior is being rejected or called into question. The approach must be caring and supportive, while establishing clear goals and boundaries. When Jesus confronted the woman caught in adultery, He was filled with compassion. However, He admonished her to "go and sin no more" (John 8:11). We must be very clear with Attendants about what must be done and the timeline for doing it. Most importantly, we must express our commitment to continuing the relationship—assuming you want to do so.

Attendants would do well in their efforts to maintain harmony and effectiveness by being less tolerant of the mediocre performance of others. Ironically, this very behavior often causes some, especially Captains, to begin to resent, lose respect for, and reject the Attendant. It becomes the paradox bemoaned by Job:

> For the thing I greatly feared has come upon me,
> And what I dreaded has happened to me.
>
> (Job 3:25)

The Captain Temperament

The Captain is the leader of the crew. The buck stops with him. Since his responsibility is to get the passengers from Point A to Point B, his chief concern must be to stay in control of the aircraft. Thus, he is more task-oriented than people-oriented. This is not to say that the Captain doesn't desire to interact with others, but given his goal, he makes the task his top priority. You will find the Captain socializing with the passengers and saying goodbye *after* the plane has landed. The mission has been accomplished.

One of the Captain's greatest personality strengths is that he is decisive. In adverse weather conditions, he decides when the "buckle your seat belt" sign will be turned on and off. He decides when the plane should go to another altitude to avoid turbulence. He can perform many functions and is not overwhelmed by a heavy workload. He is not afraid of trouble. Like Joshua and Caleb, he is ever ready to face the giants that threaten his progress. When their fellow spies became discouraged and demoralized the multitude with the news of giants in the Promised Land, these two Captains had a different response:

> But Joshua the son of Nun and Caleb the son of Jephunneh, who were among those who had spied out the land, tore their clothes; and they spoke to all the congregation of the children of Israel, saying: "The land we passed through to spy out is an exceedingly good land. If the LORD delights in us, then He will bring us into this land and give it to us, 'a land which flows with milk and honey'" (Numbers 14:6-8).

Joshua and Caleb were willing to trust God and to step out in faith. Captains are courageous and motivational.

Captains are not long-suffering with the shortcomings, incompetence, or weaknesses of others. They have low regard for those who procrastinate or who do not finish a task. The apostle Paul, a New Testament Captain, showed his intolerance by refusing to take John Mark on a second missionary trip after Mark had left him and Barnabas high and dry on the first trip (Acts 15:36-40). Captains are likely to strike your name off the list when you do not perform.

They also like to hear that they are performing well. My friend Esther Eutsey reflects this quality. She is over eighty years old and has a real Captain's personality. She is as direct in her communication style as they come. She assisted me once by inserting the ribbons in some specialty bookmarks we were developing, and she did a great job. I was not home when she dropped off the finished product, and because of my travel schedule, I did not call her for several weeks. But Captain Esther was not going to sit around and wonder what I thought about the quality of her work. After a couple of weeks, she left the following message on my answering machine. "Hello. This is Esther. I have not heard from you since I did those ribbons. Did I mess them up? Call me!"

A typical Captain. They like to know how they're doing so that they can stay in control of the situation. They do not run from confrontation nor fear a negative evaluation.

When in doubt about his or her performance, a Captain will ask for feedback. Why ponder the situation and assume the worst? You may not be as bold as my friend Esther, but at least you could ask your boss, "Do you have any suggestions for how I could improve my performance or how I could have resolved that problem more effectively?"

In a conflict, a Captain will often use a Dictator approach in order to resolve the issue. After all, Captains are usually right. Unfortunately, they sometimes forget that they are not *always* right. However, a Captain is open to a win-win negotiation if a sound and competent argument is put forth, but will resist generalizations or global statements made without support. When you confront a Captain, remember that Captains are impatient. You must get to the point quickly and not circle the airport with long, detailed explanations. The Captain needs the plane landed—now!

Although the Captain welcomes confrontation, he is the least likely of all the temperaments to be confronted since he has the most intimidating, dominant personality. The person who confronts a Captain must show respect for his authority. Since the Captain's greatest fear is losing control, he does not respond well when one challenges his authority or goes over his head. Of course, the Captain could ensure smoother interactions by being less dictatorial and domineering. He must learn to acknowledge that God has given *everyone* something of value to bring to the table. By managing his impatience, listening without interrupting, and valuing the input of others—even if it is presented in a long-drawn-out manner—the Captain will find the tension minimized in all of his relationships.

Finally, the Captain must learn to stop overstepping his boundaries.

If the limitations on his authority are unclear, he will often implement solutions and systems that he had no right to affect. Of course, he is equally frustrated by those who allow a problem to linger. He must stop trying to fix every problem he observes. He must abandon his sacred belief that "Captain knows best."

The Engineer Temperament

The flight engineer is the crew member responsible for the in-flight mechanical performance of the aircraft. His job requires much attention to detail and is critical to a successful flight. You will not find the Engineer socializing with the passengers. His focus is on the instrument panel, cabin pressurization, fuel usage, and other operating systems. He must be a perfectionist in interpreting the readings. Imagine if he were to respond to a gauge that indicated a malfunction by saying, "Oh, it'll probably be okay. No big deal." The passengers' safety would be jeopardized. You can see why the computer now performs these functions on larger planes.

The strength of the Engineer is that he is very analytical. He will tend to choose a profession that the average person finds too exacting. He sets high standards for himself and others. The Engineer spouse will often redo a household chore after the other spouse has finished the task.

My husband, Darnell, is always rearranging the dishes that I've put in the dishwasher; my goal is simply to get the door to close. We jokingly refer to each other as Oscar (me) and Felix (him) from the television sitcom *The Odd Couple*. Felix was overly neat and conscientious while Oscar was messy and disorganized. To minimize conflict in our household, we've each learned to give a little. I don't leave my high heels at the door, so Darnell has literally stopped tripping. He gives me a 30-minute warning before he comes home each day so that I have time to tidy whatever needs to be tidied. We have discussed what annoys him most, and I focus on those areas primarily. I'm actually a lot neater now, but it seems like nothing compared to his neatness.

The key to minimizing conflict with the Engineer is to understand that he simply has a need for order. Of course, he must learn that perfection is not a necessity in *every* endeavor.

Engineers are slow to make a decision. They will analyze a problem to death, agonizing over the smallest details or the simplest issues. "What shall I order to eat?" "Which color is best?" "This digital camera or that one?" On and on they go. They drive the decisive Captain crazy!

And of course, Engineers are very rules and regulations oriented. They will rarely ask anyone to make an exception to a policy. They are also reluctant to grant an exception when they have the authority to do so.

Such was the case of Esther, the Jewish queen of Persia. Mordecai, her uncle, had refused to pay honor to Haman, the king's high-ranking official, by bowing down to him as the king had commanded everyone to do. Haman had decided to retaliate by plotting the extermination of the entire Jewish population. Mordecai informed Esther of Haman's plans and asked her to go to the king, her husband, to plead for the life of her people. Her first response was that it was against the law—or "company policy"—for her to go into his presence uninvited:

> "All the king's servants and the people of the king's provinces know that any man or woman who goes into the inner court to the king, who has not been called, he has but one law: put all to death, except the one to whom the king holds out the golden scepter, that he may live. Yet I myself have not been called to go in to the king these thirty days" (Esther 4:11).

Mordecai upbraided her for her reluctance to intercede for her people.

> "Do not think in your heart that you will escape in the king's palace any more than all the other Jews. For if you remain completely silent at this time, relief and deliverance will arise for the Jews from another place, but you and your father's house will perish. Yet who knows whether you have come to the kingdom for such a time as this?" (Esther 4:13-14).

After requesting the Jews to fast with her and her maids for three days, Esther decided to risk her life by approaching the king—in spite of the law: "I will go to the king, which is against the law; and if I perish, I perish!" (Esther 4:16). Fortunately, she found favor with the king, and he accepted her request for a meeting.

Note next how methodically she handled the situation (Esther 5:1-7). She didn't rush to tell the king the reason for her coming to him. She simply invited him and Haman to dinner. At the dinner, she promised to tell him at a follow-up dinner the next day what she really wanted. Had Esther been a Captain, she would have told him the entire story the minute he extended the golden scepter. Forget dinner. No need to drag out the matter; time was wasting. But no, Engineers are thorough and systematic in their approach to life. It was at the *second* dinner that she exposed Haman's plot—right there in his presence.

> Then Queen Esther answered and said, "If I have found favor in your sight, O king, and if it pleases the king, let my life be given me at my petition, and my people at my request. For we have been sold, my people and I, to be destroyed, to be killed, and to be annihilated. Had we been sold as male and female slaves, I would have held my tongue, although the enemy could never compensate for the king's loss."
>
> So King Ahasuerus answered and said to Queen Esther, "Who is he, and where is he, who would dare presume in his heart to do such a thing?"
>
> And Esther said, "The adversary and enemy is this wicked Haman!"
>
> So Haman was terrified before the king and queen (Esther 7:3-6).

What a confrontation! The king was incensed that the wicked Haman would do such a thing. He ordered Haman to be hung, and the Jews were saved from annihilation.

You must appreciate the thoroughness of the Engineer. He takes great care to be correct, to do things the right way. His decision is not based on emotions but on facts and verifiable data. It's no wonder that his greatest fear is the fear of criticism. After all, he takes such great pains to produce perfection.

The Engineer provides the balance needed for the overly optimistic Attendant and the sometimes too-hasty Captain. It pays for these temperaments to listen to the logic of the Engineer. Of course, he must learn when enough analysis is enough. Sometimes, he has to just step out in faith as Esther did.

When in conflict with the Engineer, you must have your facts straight. Allow plenty of time for him to put forth his questions, doubts, and concerns. Give concrete reasons why you disagree with him. Do not attempt to persuade him with emotions or people-centered arguments. Your effort will yield little results. He is logic-oriented, and things must make sense.

Engineers will often find it hard to walk by faith and may miss some of the blessings that come only by stepping out in reliance on God's Word. Therefore, if you happen to be a "sense-centered" Engineer, your best strategy for a more fulfilling life is to saturate your spirit with the promises of God. Trust Him for the results.

Summary

The foregoing analysis is not intended to put anyone in a box. The temperament profile is merely a tool for understanding your own needs, fears, preferences, and propensities—and those of others. This information equips you to interact wisely and harmoniously with people who are different from you.

No one's temperament fits 100 percent into a single category. Everyone is a blend of temperaments. No category is better or worse than another; therefore, we should not exalt or esteem one above the other. Further, we must be careful not to immediately categorize a person based on our observation of a single action. Sometimes situations will dictate an individual's behavior. In a crisis, we may see an Attendant become a Captain and demand the necessary actions to resolve the problem. Therefore, it's important to look for consistent behavior over time before we attribute a personality type to anyone.

> The temperament profile is merely a tool for understanding your own needs, fears, preferences, and propensities—and those of others.

The P.A.C.E. Personality Profile Behavioral Summary in Appendix 1 sets forth the key traits of the four temperaments and will give you a quick overview and further insight into your behavioral tendencies as well as those of others.

Your objective must be to learn to accept, appreciate, and even celebrate the differences in others. In so doing, you will improve your relationships and enhance the quality of your interactions. You will also minimize the number of interpersonal conflicts that you experience and find that harmony can be achieved.

Your Challenge

Note the name of one person from each relationship listed on the following page. For each person, consider a strategy that you can employ immediately to be more effective in your interaction with him or her.

NAME	**STRATEGY**
(Example)	
Dorothy	I will patiently listen to her detailed explanations without interruption.

Friend:

_____   _____

Relative:

_____   _____

Coworker:

_____   _____

Other:

_____   _____

Which personality type do you most enjoy interacting with?
_____. Why?

Which personality type is the most difficult for you to interact with? _____. Why?

What weaknesses in your personality are you willing to confess to the Lord and allow Him to change?

Part 5

Confrontation Guidelines
for Selected Situations

15

Family Interactions

Now it's time to practice what you have learned. Below are several common conflicts that may crop up in your interactions with family members, and some suggested guidelines for resolving them. Though the specific situations may not exactly mirror your own, the principles will still apply.

Situation: The Unsupportive Husband

Your husband works hard at his job each day. You also work hard each day, whether at the office or at home. When he comes home, he grabs the sports section of the newspaper and waits for you to finish making dinner. After dinner, you clean the kitchen and help little Johnny with his homework. You finally make it to bed dead tired while your husband settles in to watch the news. You resent that he won't help out. You've tolerated his insensitivity ever since Johnny was born. It's time to deal with the situation.

Resolution Guidelines:

- Don't resort to passive-aggressive behavior—sulking and moodiness—hoping he'll figure out what's wrong.
- Tell him how much you appreciate what he does already (for

example, being financially responsible). Use lots of bread in the confrontation "sandwich." Most men respond favorably to appreciation.

- Don't accuse him of being insensitive. By doing everything yourself in the past, you may have taught him that it was okay not to help. He's not a mind reader. (Yes, I know. He's not blind either.)

- Be clear about what you want from him. Give him *options* on specific tasks—washing dishes, bathing the child, doing laundry, paying bills—so that he doesn't think you're being a whining nag.

- Stay calm. It may have taken you quite some time to muster up the courage to confront; don't blow it now.

- Subsequently acknowledge and express appreciation for any improvement.

Situation: Siblings Sharing Mom's Care

Your aging mother divorced your father many years ago. Her monthly Social Security check is not sufficient to cover all her current financial requirements. You have four siblings, three of whom are very responsible, although not as financially secure as you, the attorney. Your brother, Ron, does odd jobs from time to time, but he's supported primarily by his live-in girlfriend.

You have called the rest of your siblings with a request for support for your mother. Everyone, except Ron, has agreed to $150 per month. Ron says he can't commit to a specific amount because his earnings are sporadic. He says that whenever he has a little extra money, he'll take it to her.

You disapprove of every aspect of Ron's life. You wonder if he will ever grow up. You're feeling angry that his commitment is so vague. You've decided that he must commit to something more definite, and you call him back to tell him so.

Resolution Guidelines:

- Maintain a positive attitude. Do not refer to his irresponsibility or to his lifestyle. Stick to the issue at hand—getting support for your mother, not changing his ways.

- Ask him what minimum financial commitment he could make to the support-money pool.

- If he insists that he cannot contribute, try to negotiate a nonfinancial commitment. For example, since his schedule is flexible, ask him if he would commit two days a week to take her to the doctor or to run other errands or to just sit with her for awhile.

- Don't brag or whine that you will be required to cover the lion's share of the budget. He may resent you.

- Tell him how much you and his mother will appreciate whatever effort he puts forth.

Situation: The Half-Truth and Nothing But

Your husband, Robert, a corporate manager, told you that he was taking Jim and Molly to lunch to show his appreciation for their assistance to his department during a recent government audit. You thought nothing of it until later when he mentioned that the service had been good and that the *four* of them had thoroughly enjoyed the food. With your normal curiosity, you ask who the fourth person was. He sheepishly admits that his attractive assistant manager, Lula, had also joined them. Now you're upset, not because she joined them, but because Robert felt the need to hide it. Until this point in your 20-year marriage, he has never given you a reason to doubt his integrity. But now you wonder.

Resolution Guidelines:

- Take a deep breath and ask the Holy Spirit to calm your emotions.

- Don't immediately accuse Robert of having an affair with Lula.

- Ask Robert why he felt the need to hide the truth. Listen carefully to his explanation.

- Ask yourself if, perhaps, you've expressed an inordinate amount of jealousy that could have caused Robert to fear your response had you known the truth.

- Let him know the impact the lie has had upon you (for example, disappointment or loss of trust).

- Make a decision to forgive him. Helpful hint: Extend to him the grace that God has extended to you for your trespasses!

- Do not rehearse the incident each time Robert doesn't do what you ask.

Situation: The Spendthrift Teenager

You give your sixteen-year-old son an allowance on the first and fifteenth of each month. Since he started dating a girl from an affluent family, he always seems to need a little extra cash prior to the next allowance date. The first couple of times he asked, you obliged him. However, you realize that you are hindering him from learning how to manage his money. You have been a good single parent and prefer not to have any tension in the relationship. But love has to be tough.

Resolution Guidelines:

- Tell your son, in a matter-of-fact tone, that you love him too much to continue to bridge his financial gaps.

- Stick to your guns; let him reap the consequences of overspending.

- Suggest that he find low-cost ways to entertain his new flame.

- Encourage him to look for a part-time job.

Situation: The Babysitting-Weary Grandma

Grandma, you've just hung up from a conversation with your son, who announced that he'd be bringing the kids over for the weekend. He and his wife are going to Las Vegas to have a little fun. Last weekend his old chums from college were in town, and he needed you to babysit then, also. Since your husband's death, they have assumed that you have nothing else to do. You didn't mean it literally when you said you're always available. In fact, you recently joined a support group at church and have been looking forward to the planned activities. You rarely have the time to babysit at all anymore. Confront your son.

Resolution Guidelines:

- Reiterate how much you love your grandchildren.

- Express your excitement over your new extracurricular activities and the commitment that you've made to pursue them to the fullest.

- Admit responsibility for creating the situation that is now troubling you.

- Express your intent to retire from babysitting except for when it's convenient for you.

- Abandon the fear that he will retaliate by refusing to let you see the grandchildren; you'll always be the most trusted babysitter.

16

Marketplace Interactions

Ask anyone who has worked in an office or other business environment, and she will tell you that the workplace is where you will see the drama of every temperament played out daily. The scenarios below are a sampling of typical situations that may arise in your work or professional settings. I have suggested some general guidelines for dealing with each. Timing is important in confronting the issues in order to clarify goals and objectives and to minimize your stress.

Situation: The Overworked Assistant

You were recently hired to work for a small accounting firm. The pay is great and the three partners are all wonderful Christians. Yesterday was the first day of the busy season. Each partner, all with Captain temperaments, has given you a list of tasks to perform. Clearly, you will not be able to complete all of them in the allotted time. In addition, you won't be able to work much overtime since your husband recently had major surgery and is still immobile. You understand the personality types, and you already know that the three partners, although Christians, will be unsympathetic to personal woes that take you away from work.

Resolution Guidelines:

- Ask for clarity on who your immediate boss is and whose work has priority.

- Thoroughly review the tasks to get an estimate of the time required to complete them.

- Ask your immediate boss to rank or approve *your* ranking of the priorities. Caution: Don't get frustrated if the boss deems a task more important than you think it should be. Submit to his or her authority. Remember that the buck doesn't stop with you.

- Be as flexible as your home life permits. If you can come in for a half-day on Saturday or work two hours extra on Wednesday, do so.

- If the busy season never seems to end, ask God to open another door of employment. Your employer is not your source of employment, but a chosen channel for a chosen season.

Situation: The Unprofessional Boss

Your boss has no people skills. She confronts her staff openly and loudly. This is a real deal-breaker for you. Before you joined the company several months ago as a level-one project manager, you specifically asked if employees were treated with dignity and respect. She had assured you that was the case.

This morning at the weekly staff meeting, she had a hostile confrontation with one of the project managers. She humiliated him while the rest of the staff sat in stony silence. You recognize her need for salvation, and so you patiently "look beyond her faults and see her needs." However, you have decided that she should be advised of how her behavior is affecting staff morale as well as the company's image.

Resolution Guidelines:

- Invite her to a private location to discuss the matter since she may become hostile and embarrass you as well. Know that there is a risk in confronting. In admonishing us to confront, Jesus knew that it may not always go smoothly: "Moreover if your brother sins against you, go and tell him his fault between you and him alone. *If* he hears you, you have gained your brother. But *if* he will not hear..." (Matthew 18:15-16).

- Use the sandwich approach discussed earlier.

    Bread: Thank her for agreeing to talk to you. Tell her the strengths you have observed in her. Mention anything else that you can sincerely compliment about her work skills (things you have learned from her, for example).

    Meat: While you have not personally experienced her wrath, own the problem anyway. You may be next! Describe a specific situation that you witnessed in which she behaved in an unprofessional manner. Explain how you feel when another employee is humiliated. Be careful not to use judgmental statements or phrases, such as "you always..." or "you never..."

    Bread: Reaffirm your commitment to support her personally as well as to support the company objectives.

- Thank her for being willing to listen to you.

Situation: Merit Raise Denied

Your merit raise has been denied for three years straight. You know you're doing a good job, and you've trained over half the people in your department. In addition, you experienced an unexpected financial reversal in the past month, and your savings are just about depleted. You could use the extra money. You plan to confront the boss to find out what has held up your increase.

Resolution Guidelines:

- Keep a personal record of your achievements on the job; refer to them when you present your request for more money.

- Never ask for a raise based on your financial obligations. Raises should be based on the value of the job and your performance.

- If your request is denied, ask for specific recommendations on what you need to do for your request to be granted later. Agree on the time period for what will be considered "later."

- Pray and expect God to move on your behalf and to give you favor with your superiors.

Situation: Sexual Harassment

You are being sexually harassed by a manager from another department who is part of the good-old-boys' network. He plays tennis with your boss twice a week. His advances started a couple of weeks ago when he took a long, desiring look at you at the water cooler. You believe you should nip this in the bud before it goes any further.

Resolution Guidelines:

- Ask the Holy Spirit to give you words that will have the most impact.

- Approach him in his office while he is alone. Remain standing.

- Forget the sandwich approach and get right to the meat of the matter. "You may not be aware of it, but your behavior toward me constitutes sexual harassment." Looking directly into his eyes with a sober expression, emphatically state, "It must stop. If such behavior continues, I will have to report it." Use whatever specific words God has given you.

- If the harasser doesn't take you seriously, or if he attempts to minimize your concern, assure him that you will take the issue to the next level. Remember that you are not trying to preserve a relationship here.

17

Social and Other
Interactions

I n this final section on practicing what you've learned, we turn to those relationships you have that add fun or improve the quality of your life. For sure, you have no desire to tolerate unnecessary drama or other relational problems from them. Try responding to these scenarios without first looking at the suggested guidelines and see how your responses compare.

Situation: Sharing the Bill

Every Friday evening, you and several of your friends meet at a local restaurant for dinner. You always seem to end up paying a disproportionate share of the bill. Why just last week, after the tab was divided equally, your share was $25, and you had ordered only a $7 bowl of soup!

You're beginning to resent that some in the group order expensive appetizers, extra drinks, and dessert. You want to continue these get-togethers, but you'd prefer to pay for your food separately. You've kept quiet until now for fear the others would call you "cheap" if you were to request a separate check.

Resolution Guidelines:

- First be aware that some restaurants will not give separate checks for a party of five or more.

- Take enough cash to pay only for what you plan to order and a generous tip.

- Announce lightheartedly before orders are taken that you're going to be a better manager of your money (or your diet) and will be spending only a certain amount. Therefore, you're having the _____.

- When the bill arrives, try to get to it first to confirm the accuracy of your charges. Place the appropriate amount, including taxes and tip, on the table. Politely ignore any attempts to saddle you with more of the bill. If you're really uncomfortable, excuse yourself from the table to go to the restroom after you place your funds on the table and leave the rest of the group to figure out their share of the bill. If you're paying by credit card along with others who are paying their share with a credit card, simply tell the server how much to charge to your card. I do this often and it's pretty hassle free.

Situation: "I Hate My Entrée!"

This month's budget finally allows you to have dinner at a certain upscale restaurant. You order the day's special at the suggestion of your waiter. After the first bite of the dish, you realize it's not what you expected. It's much too rich for your diet. You feel bad about this because the waiter has been so nice. However, you've made a commitment to abandon your Abdicator conflict-management style, so you've decided to return the entrée.

Resolution Guidelines:

- Don't delay. I know a woman who, upon consuming an entire stack of pancakes, demanded that they be taken off her check. She alleged they were burned! The waiter could not find one shred of evidence to support her claim.

- Quietly explain to the waiter why you are returning the dish.

- Don't be hostile toward the waiter because of your disappointment; he didn't prepare the food.

- Before you order the replacement dish, ask how it is prepared and how patrons have responded to it.

Situation: The Ungrateful Guests

You are a budding speaker, writer, or other professional. During the past month, you attended several expensive seminars on how to be more successful in your profession. You invite a small group of ladies with similar aspirations to your home to share with them the valuable insights you've gained from the seminars. You serve a light lunch and also hand out printed materials that you put together. They all thank you for your kindness as they leave the house. However, only two of them send a thank-you note to formally express their appreciation. You're perturbed by the lack of manners of the ones who didn't send a card or even call. You're debating whether to tell them how you feel about their behavior.

Resolution Guidelines:

- Ask yourself what your real motive was for inviting them over. Was it to show off or to share information?

- Realize that not everyone shares your grace or manners. The behavior of these women does not mean they were ungrateful. They probably had no inkling that they offended you. Remind yourself that, "A man's wisdom gives him patience; it is to his glory to overlook an offense" (Proverbs 19:11 NIV). So forget about it! This is not a pattern of behavior that will affect the ongoing quality of your life.

Situation: The Incompetent Pastor

You belong to a small church that is part of a democratically run denomination. The pastor assigned to the church by headquarters is not working out. His sermons are boring and uninspiring. He has no vision for the church and no burden for the surrounding community—spiritually or socially. Furthermore, he's in poor health.

You are a member of several prominent committees, but not the committee responsible for the removal of the pastor. You have an open, honest, and supportive relationship with the pastor. However, you believe you would incur the wrath of God for "touching his anointed" if you were to participate on any level in helping to remove him.

The pastoral committee has taken an ostrich stance—burying their heads in the sand—and has joined the rest of the congregation in murmuring about his incompetence and in wishing that he would resign.

Resolution Guidelines:

- Resist the temptation to join the murmuring.

- Ask God if He is calling you to be the pastor's "Samuel" (see 1 Samuel 3:11-18) by telling him how he is affecting the congregation.

- If God gives you the green light to discuss the matter with the pastor, own the problem when you meet with him. State how his performance has affected you personally, as well as the other members.

- Don't demand his resignation. Stay in your role as a messenger.

- If the pastor doesn't resign, or you see no improvement over a reasonable period of time, look for another church. Your spiritual well-being is in jeopardy.

Situation: The Fornicating Deacon

You, the pastor, have heard that, Jim, cochairman of the deacon board, has moved in with his girlfriend. Jim has been a faithful tither and a good leader. You have noticed, however, that his attendance at the weekly deacons' meetings has been sporadic. He also seems to have lost some of his zeal for the Lord. As the pastor, you believe you must address this matter right away to minimize further negative impact on Jim and on the congregation.

Resolution Guidelines:

- Call Jim and set a time to meet with him right away.
- Don't accuse him of being guilty. Instead, ask if the rumor is true.
- If he admits to the wrongdoing, explain to him the previously decided consequences, which should include the immediate relinquishment of his leadership position, submission to spiritual counseling, and other appropriate measures. (You may also consider requiring him to confess his sin to the church since it is public knowledge.)
- Express your desire and commitment to see him restored to a right relationship with God and with the church.
- Know that your stock will rise in the eyes of the congregation when they see you exercising the courage to confront a thorny issue.

Situation: A Leeching Friend

A relative or friend has borrowed money from you and has conveniently forgotten to repay you—again. You resent that she lives above her means while you often forego certain pleasures to save money. She now finds herself in another financial jam. She asks you if she can "borrow a little change." You have decided to put a stop to it.

Resolution Guidelines:

- Be a broken record in saying no.

- Realize that by always bailing the person out, you are enabling her to remain irresponsible.

- Don't leave the door open for a future request by saying you don't have the money *this time.*

- Refuse to be manipulated or made to feel guilty.

Situation: The Immodest Friend

Lucy accepted the Lord and joined the church last year. Since then, she and you have attended various functions together and occasionally enjoy girl talk on the phone. Lucy is a real knockout; she has it, and she flaunts it. Some of her outfits are downright indecent, but she wears them to church anyway.

She is the focus of attention wherever she goes. Even the highly spiritual men struggle to keep from eyeing her. You want to see her mature in the Lord and to be more modest in her dress. You've decided that it's time to discuss this with her.

Resolution Guidelines:

- Not so fast! Have you earned the right to delve into such a sensitive area of her life? Does she know that you genuinely care?

- How much do you know about any issues from her past that could have caused her to think that dressing this way is the only way to be valued?

- If you honestly believe you have earned the right to speak of this matter, start by asking her some nonaccusatory questions, such: "Have you noticed how the way you dress affects the men of the church? Perhaps this is a blind spot, and if so, I care enough to make you aware of it." Or, "What do you suppose God thinks about how you dress? Did you ask Him?"

- You may want to share a past struggle that you've overcome so you don't come across as self-righteous.

- You may consider giving her a book on modesty or sharing with her the Scriptures on this subject.

- Reaffirm your commitment to maintaining a mutually beneficial relationship.

A Confrontation Gone Wrong

Background: Connie hears rumors that her brother George is allowing undesirable characters to crash at the home he occupies with their elderly mother, Grace. The household is supported by Grace's Social Security income and occasional contributions from the seven remaining siblings. Under a special government-funded program, George is paid a monthly stipend to be Grace's caregiver. George is also a drug abuser—which explains why he does not have a "real" job. Unfortunately, he is the only sibling available to help Grace in this manner since she requires 24-hour care.

Connie's other siblings are aware of the stream of shady visitors to Grace's home and other problems, but they have no intention of confronting George because he has an explosive temper, and they'd rather just keep quiet for peace sake. Connie, a high-achieving go-getter, is not intimidated by anyone. She is known to confront issues head on and to effect a quick resolution. She decides to pay George a visit.

Connie: "George, I hear that you're allowing thugs to spend the night in this house. Why in the world are you putting Mom in harm's way? You don't own this place and you have no right to allow anybody to crash here. Are you crazy?"

George: "What are you talking about? And what if I do let a friend spend the night occasionally? At least I'm here with Mom. You're too busy to even come over here more than once a month. If you don't like what I do, tough! All you do is

complain and criticize! I don't have to listen to this madness."
Storms out and slams the door.

Confrontation Analysis

Even though Connie did the right thing by confronting George,
she did not get the desired results: a commitment from George to
change his behavior. What principles of effective confrontation did
she violate?

> "Negatively labeling someone's personality
> certainly forces them into a defensive position,
> because the negative label attacks the other's
> personal need for a positive self-image."

First, Connie made an accusation based upon hearsay. She failed
to ask George if the story were true. Second, she eroded his dignity
when she reminded him of the obvious—that he did not own the
house. George probably beats himself daily about his plight. Finally,
she negatively labeled his personhood by asking "Are you crazy?" In
his book, *Managing Interpersonal Conflict*, William A. Donohue warns,
"Negatively labeling someone's personality certainly forces them into
a defensive position, because the negative label attacks the other's
personal need for a positive self-image. In fact, few people like to
have others evaluate their personality because such evaluations are like
saying, 'You're bad, and you can't do anything about it.'"[5]

George was hurt by her remarks and retaliated—a natural response
when attacked. He reminded her that Grace was obviously a low priority on her schedule. He attempted to level the playing field by running
a guilt trip on Connie.

What if Connie had tried a more positive approach? Let's imagine
what the outcome might have been.

Connie: "George, I appreciate your taking care of Mom. Because
of you, she gets to live at home instead of a nursing home. [This

is the bread of the sandwich approach discussed in Chapter 9.]
I'd like to talk to you about some rumors I've heard regarding
undesirables spending the night here. Is this true?"

George: "Yes, it's true. A couple of my buddies have gotten
kicked out by their girlfriends or family members, or are just
down on their luck. I let them spend a night or two here until
things blow over at home. These guys have stood by me and
allowed me to crash at their places when you've kicked me
out of this house. I can't turn my back on them. They're not
hurting anybody by spending the night here."

Connie (in a calm voice)*:* "George, I know that you have a big
heart and have a hard time saying no to people in distress.
You and Mom are very much alike in that way and it's an
admirable trait [More bread...very important; here comes
the meat.]

"Unfortunately, this situation cannot be allowed. It not only
threatens Mom's safety, but it also jeopardizes the financial
support you receive for caring for her. The state will declare
her ineligible for in-home caregiver benefits if they learn that
others stay here from time to time. As Mom's conservator,
I'm asking you not to allow anyone to spend the night here
ever again. If you do, I'll be forced to ask you to move. I'll
hire another person to live here and take care of Mom.

"If her support is discontinued, she'll have to live in a nursing home, and you'll be forced to find somewhere else to
live. When your friends come knocking at the door, just use
me as the scapegoat and explain that you'd like to help, but
you'll face dire consequences if you do. [Now more bread...
very important; it's a sandwich remember?] Don't do this to
yourself, George. We need you and Mom needs you."

I'd venture to say that with this approach, where the tone is encouraging and nonaccusing, George's response will be much more positive
than his response to the initial confrontation that was fraught with
accusation and hostility.

Epilogue

Confrontation carries a risk. Jesus acknowledged that when He commanded us to confront those who have wronged us. "Moreover if your brother sins against you, go and tell him his fault between you and him alone. If he hears you, you have gained your brother. But *if* he will not hear, take with you one or two more, that 'by the mouth of two or three witnesses every word may be established'" (Matthew 18:15-16).

You may follow all the principles of effective confrontation discussed in this book and still not get the desired response. This does not mean that the confrontation failed. You are not responsible for someone else's response. You've planted the seed; you cannot make it grow. You've obeyed God; the rest is up to Him.

Once you learn to confront personal offenses and stop being a victim, you'll feel empowered. You'll stop having conversations with yourself about what you should have said or beating yourself because you didn't speak up. Your self-esteem will increase and you will gain the respect of others. However, others may initially be put off by your new behavior.

I heard Dr. James Dobson, the popular Christian psychologist, say that he once told his young outspoken son, "When you say what you really mean, some people will think you're really mean." That's why it's important to get God's words so that you may speak with the "tongue of the learned" (Isaiah 50:4). There is never a need to be offensive. However, some people may be offended or even hurt by the truth you share with them. Like surgery, confrontation is often accompanied by pain. Job declared, "How painful are honest words!" (Job 6:25 NIV).

"When you say what you really mean, some people will think you're really mean."

Confrontation is necessary for growth. If we care, we will confront and believe God for a favorable outcome. So the next time you're tempted to suffer in silence, to swallow your rage, to explode, to retreat, or to bury your head in the sand, stop and plan an effective confrontation.

Aristotle said, "Anyone can become angry—that is easy. But to be angry with the right person, to the right degree, at the right time, for the right purpose, and in the right way—that is not easy."

The good news is that you do not have to rely on your own strength to abate your anger. Neither must you depend on your own ingenuity to bring peace into a situation. Our Lord has given us a mandate to initiate reconciliation whether we are the offended or the offender. Only an effective confrontation will bridge the gap between conflict and cooperation, between hurt and harmony. Through the application of God's Word, you can confront effectively without offending.

P.A.C.E. Personality Profile
Behavioral Summary

	PASSENGER	ATTENDANT
Behavior pattern:	Open/Indirect	Open/Direct
Known for:	Steadiness/Loyalty	Friendliness
Fears:	Change	Disapproval
Needs/Seeks:	Security	Recognition
Pace:	Slow/Easy	Fast/Spontaneous
Priority:	Maintaining relationships	Relationships/Interacting
Appearance:	Casual, conforming	Fashionable, stylish
Work Environment:	Personal, relaxed, friendly, informal	Stimulating, personal, cluttered, friendly
Under pressure will:	Submit/Acquiesce	Attack/Be sarcastic
Gains security by:	Close relationships	Flexibility

	PASSENGER	**ATTENDANT**
Wants to maintain:	Relationships	Status
Needs others to support their:	Feelings	Ideas
Achieves acceptance by:	Conformity, loyalty	Playfulness, stimulating environment
Likes you to be:	Pleasant	Fun
Wants to be:	Liked	Accepted
Irritated by:	Insensitivity, impatience	Boredom, routine
Measures personal worth by:	Compatibility with others/ Depth of relationships	Acknowledgement, recognition, compliments
Familiar expression:	"Wait"	"Yes"
Decisions are:	Considered	Spontaneous

	CAPTAIN	**ENGINEER**
Behavior pattern:	Self-sufficient/Direct	Self-contained/Indirect
Known for:	Dominance	Compliance
Fears:	Loss of control	Criticism
Needs/Seeks:	Productivity	Accuracy
Pace:	Fast/Hurried	Slow/Systematic
Priority:	The Task/Results	The Task/Process

	CAPTAIN	ENGINEER
Appearance:	Businesslike, functional	Formal, conservative
Work-space:	Formal, efficient, structured	Structured, organized, functional, formal
Under pressure will:	Dictate/Assert	Withdraw/Avoid
Gains security by:	Control	Preparation
Wants to maintain:	Success	Credibility
Needs others to support their:	Goals	Logic, facts
Achieves acceptance by:	Leadership, competition	Correctness, thoroughness
Likes you to be:	To the point	Precise
Wants to be:	In charge	Correct
Irritated by:	Inefficiency, indecision	Surprises, unpredictability
Measures personal worth by:	Results, measurable progress	Precision, accuracy,
Familiar expression:	"Next"	"Maybe"
Decisions are:	Quick	Deliberate

Appendix 2

Index to Biblical Conflicts

Endnotes

1. John Bevere, *The Bait of Satan* (Lake Mary, FL: Charisma House, 1997), 3.

2. Stephen R. Covey, *The Seven Habits of Highly Effective People* (New York: Simon and Schuster, 1990), 219.

3. M. Scott Peck, *The Road Less Traveled* (New York: Simon and Schuster, 1979), 16.

4. The name *Sarai* may mean "ruler, captain, or governor" (the commentators do not all agree on this). True to her name, Sarai began to dictate what course of action she and Abram should take. Later, God changed her name to Sarah (Genesis 17:15), which means "princess."

5. William A. Donohue with Robert Kolt, *Managing Interpersonal Conflict* (Newbury Park, CA: Sage Publications, 1992), 44.

How to Contact
the Author

Deborah Smith Pegues is an experienced certified public accountant, a Bible teacher, a speaker, a certified behavioral consultant specializing in understanding personality temperaments, and the author of *30 Days to Taming Your Tongue, 30 Days to Taming Your Stress, 30 Days to Taming Your Finances, Supreme Confidence,* and *Socially Smart in 60 Seconds.* She and her husband, Darnell, have been married for almost 30 years and make their home in California.

For speaking engagements, please contact the author at:

> The Pegues Group
> P.O. Box 56382
> Los Angeles, California 90056
> (323) 293-5861

> or

> E-mail: ddpegues@sbcglobal.net
> www.confrontingissues.com

30 DAYS TO TAMING YOUR TONGUE

What You Say (and Don't Say) Will Improve Your Relationships

Deborah Smith Pegues

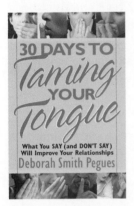

Certified behavioral consultant Deborah Pegues knows how easily a slip of the tongue can cause problems in personal and business relationships. This is why she wrote the popular *30 Days to Taming Your Tongue* (280,000 copies sold). Now in trade size, Pegues' 30-day devotional will help each reader not only tame their tongue but make it productive rather than destructive.

With humor and a bit of refreshing sass, Deborah devotes chapters to learning how to overcome the

- Retaliating Tongue
- Know-It-All Tongue
- Belittling Tongue
- Hasty Tongue
- Gossiping Tongue
- 25 More!

Short stories, anecdotes, soul-searching questions, and scripturally based personal affirmations combine to make each applicable and life changing.

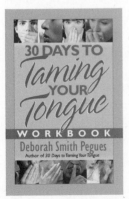

30 DAYS TO TAMING YOUR TONGUE WORKBOOK

If you're one of the thousands of readers who's found help in *30 Days to Taming Your Tongue*, this hands-on guide will help you keep on doing what you've been learning.

30 DAYS TO IMPROVING YOUR ATTITUDE

Deborah Smith Pegues

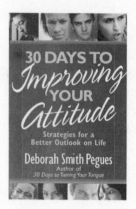

From Deborah Pegues, popular author of the bestselling *30 Days to Taming Your Tongue,* comes a powerful guide for conquering those bad attitudes that can derail your personal and professional relationships. Here's just a sampling of the attitudes Pegues tackles head on:

- condescendsion
- control
- intolerance
- judgmentalism
- self-centeredness

Scripture-based principles, heart-searching personal challenges, and healing prayers and affirmations will point readers toward the path to a new attitude.

30 DAYS TO TAMING YOUR STRESS

Deborah Smith Pegues

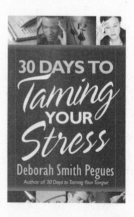

Are you sleeping well at night? Finding enough time in the day to do the things you enjoy? Sometimes stress causes us to miss out on the rest, fun, and health we long for. But you truly can tame this unruly taskmaster in 30 short days.

With insight gleaned from her experience as a behavioral consultant, Deborah Pegues will help you learn how to change self-sabotaging behavior, enjoy the present, evaluate your expectations, and release your tension.

SUPREME CONFIDENCE

DEBORAH SMITH PEGUES

Supreme Confidence uses biblical and modern-day examples to help you recognize and overcome insecurity's many guises. Strategies such as resting in God's Word, resisting intimidation, and remembering past victories provide an effective plan of attack on self-doubt. Beyond that, you'll discover how to establish boundaries, conquer perfectionism, empower others, and embrace success.

You can understand and overcome the core fears that limit you. And you can build the confidence you need to enjoy life at home, at work, and at play!

EMERGENCY PRAYERS

DEBORAH SMITH PEGUES

We need God's help...and fast! Deborah Smith Pegues offers readers a 9-1-1 prayerbook for life's many circumstances and needs. Brief, and heartfelt, these prayers bring God's Word to the forefront of a reader's mind as they lift up cries for:

- help on the homefront
- resistance of temptations
- guidance in important decisions
- comfort in the midst of pain

SOCIALLY SMART IN 60 SECONDS

Etiquette Dos and Don'ts for Personal and Professional Success

DEBORAH SMITH PEGUES

Deborah Pegues offers 60-second etiquette solutions for awkward pauses, social situations, and everyday encounters. While other books focus on doing things right, Deborah shares how to do the right thing as she presents simple ways for readers to

- make proper and inviting introductions
- scribe personable emails, letters, and thank-you notes
- understand and be mindful of intercultural dos and don'ts
- host events, dinners, and overnight guests with ease

For everything from networking to dating to tipping, this quick and thorough guide helps readers turn their thoughts to the needs of others and practice courtesy and consideration anytime.

FINANCIAL SURVIVAL IN UNCERTAIN TIMES

Deborah Smith Pegues

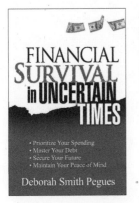

Amid the confusion, anger, and anxiety surrounding the U.S. economic crisis, Deborah Pegues offers proven strategies and wise counsel for financial survival. Drawing on more than three decades of professional experience as a certified public accountant, Pegues will show readers how to

- arm themselves with the information they need to make wise decisions
- prioritize and control spending and get out of debt
- find low-cost alternatives and cultivate contentment
- maintain quality of life amidst the economic turmoil

Soul-searching questions and biblical principles combine to fill each chapter with hope for financial health in the midst of uncertain times.